The Perfect Portfolio

For Artists And Writers

How To Put Together A Creative "Book" That Sells

Other Helpful Books
Available From
The Career Press:

Your First Resume (Fry)

Your First Interview (Fry)

The Write Stuff (Bjelland)

From Campus to Corporation (Strasser/Sena)

Transitions (Strasser/Sena)

The Perfect Portfolio

For Artists And Writers

How To Put Together A Creative "Book" That Sells

By Marilyn Seguin

THE CAREER PRESS
62 BEVERLY RD.,
PO BOX 34
HAWTHORNE, NJ 07507
1-800-CAREER-1
201-427-0229 (OUTSIDE U.S.)
FAX: 201-427-2037

THE PERFECT PORTFOLIO For Artists and Writers: How To Put Together A Creative "Book" That Sells
ISBN 0-934829-68-3, $10.95

Cover design by Jinny Bastianelli,
The Electronic Studio

All photographs courtesy of Rick Zaiden

List of ten proofreading tips (Chapter 4) excerpted from "Spellbinding Typos: How to Avoid Those Typeuh-ohs," by Marilyn Seguin, printed in the June/July 1987 issue of *The Professional Communicator* and reprinted with permission of its publisher, Women in Communications, Inc.

Questions from the Lindquist/Endicott Report (Chapter 5) reprinted with permission of Victor R. Lindquist, Associate Dean/Director, The Placement Center, Northwestern University.

Copies of this volume may be ordered by mail or phone directly from the publisher. To order by mail, please include price as noted above, $2.50 handling per order, plus $1.00 for each book ordered. Send to: The Career Press Inc., 62 Beverly Rd., PO Box 34, Hawthorne, NJ 07507

Or call Toll-Free 1-800-CAREER-1 (in Canada: 201-427-0229) to order using your VISA or Mastercard or for further information on all books published or distributed by The Career Press.

Dedication

To my students at The University of Akron, who gave me the inspiration;

To my husband, Rollie, who gave me the encouragement;

And to my children, Scott and Katy, who gave me the peace and quiet I needed to complete this book.

Table of Contents

The Perfect Portfolio

Table of Photographs

The Perfect Portfolio

extra resumes. Flat items can be presented on the
loose-leaf pages, protected by a nylon or acetate
sleeve. These portfolio cases come in an assortment
of sizes and colors.

Page 53

This photographer's portfolio contains images in a
variety of formats, including a proof sheet and an
enlargement of a selected shot. (Materials from the
portfolio of Rick Zaidan.)

Page 55

A photographer's portfolio ready for mailing to an
out-of-town employer is well-protected. Slides are inserted into a vinyl slide sheet, sandwiched between
two pieces of cardboard, and mailed along with a
self-addressed stamped envelope.

Page 57

This photographer's portfolio displays a black-and-
white enlargement and a tear sheet from the publication in which the photo was published. (Materials
from the portfolio of Rick Zaidan.)

Page 59

These large color transparencies, mounted between
two pieces of black mat board, are ready for viewing
over a light table. (Transparencies from the portfolio
of Rick Zaidan.)

Page 61

This graphic designer's portfolio includes a paragraph of description on the page facing each design.
When presenting the portfolio in person, the
designer removes the paragraph and explains
everything the interviewer needs to know about each
piece. (Poster from the portfolio of Bruce Morrill.)

Page 63

This graphic designer's portfolio displays several pieces from a single campaign. These pieces were created by a student for a class project, and although they were never printed, these samples showcase the designer's talent and skill. (Designs from the portfolio of Michelle Palko.)

Page 65

This writer's portfolio binder didn't have sewn-in pockets for loose items. The writer made a pocket by cutting away the top half of the protective acetate sheet that covered the loose-leaf page.

Acknowledgements

Thank You!

The information in this book was compiled from interviews and discussions with a wide variety of educators, career counselors and employers of communicators and visual artists, as well as hundreds of job-seeking students at The University of Akron and Kent State University.

Members of the Akron Chapter of Women in Communications, Inc., and of The University of Akron Student Chapter of IABC, the International Association of Business Communicators, were also helpful.

I wish to especially thank and acknowledge the following individuals for their advice and support in the research and writing of this book: Barbara Hipsman, Timothy Smith, Gregory Blase, Zoe McCathrin, Ann Schierhorn, and Gregory Moore of the School of Journalism and Mass Communication, Kent State University; John Buchanan and Bruce Morrill of the School of Art, Kent State University; Kathleen Endres, Department of Communication, The University of Akron; Henry Ruminski, Department of Communication, Wright State University; Pamela VanDe-Weert, Career Planning and Placement Center, Kent State

University; Phyllis Madan, Career Development and Placement Office, Fashion Institute of Technology, State University of New York; Marilyn Carrell, Office of Career Planning and Placement, the University of Akron; John Dages, assistant managing editor, Crain Communications; Dale Allen, editor, *Akron Beacon Journal;* Beverly Pierce, Employee Communications, The BF Goodrich Company; Sharon Feador, Personnel, Edgell Communications.

Introduction

Yes, Your Portfolio
Can Be Perfect

This Book Will Show You How

Most job seekers think that writing and designing their resume and putting together individual cover letters, the traditional means by which employers use to screen applicants, are the key steps in the job search process.

They are. But for those of you seeking jobs in the fields of communications or visual arts, a resume and cover letter are *not enough*. For you, a portfolio—a selected sampling of your best writing, artwork, photography, etc.—is not just an important job-search tool, it's an *essential* one.

I am a writer. My own first portfolio was nothing more than a notebook containing two stories published in my college newspaper and a contact sheet from a photography class. Rough as it was, it won me an entry-level job writing scripts for a nonprofit agency. In its various incarnations, my portfolio has since landed me assignments as feature writer, publicity writer, newsletter editor, columnist and, with this book, first-time author!

I wrote this book so that anybody—no matter how small their pile of samples, how limited their experience, how inexpensive the portfolio case they can afford—can construct and organize a job-winning portfolio. Guaranteed.

This Book's For You

The Perfect Portfolio was written for anyone preparing for a career in any communications or visual arts occupation. High school or college students seeking their first job do, after all, have the hardest time putting a portfolio together—there just doesn't seem to be enough work to include!

This book will help even the least-experienced students learn how to arrange samples (and, more importantly, where to get them!), but it is certainly not exclusively for recent college graduates.

The Perfect Portfolio is also an essential guidebook for those of you already working in these fields who, for one reason or another, never collected your work samples into portfolio format...or never did it *right*. Learning how to correctly organize your portfolio—what to include, what not to include, how to order your samples, etc.—so that it *sells* you and your work might well be your secret weapon when you change jobs or position yourself for a raise or promotion with your existing employer.

A portfolio is also essential for freelance communicators and visual artists who must display their previous work in order to win new clients. A portfolio of work samples is an instrument that proves the freelancer's competence and ability to command a professional fee for his or her work.

For all of you, *The Perfect Portfolio* is the book you need to guide you through the pitfalls of the job search process, help you assemble your work samples into an attractive, job-winning portfolio, and land exactly the job you want!

Chapter 1

Getting Ready To Get Ready

The Power Of A Portfolio

Journalists sometimes call them "string books." Ad people just call them "books." In this volume, we'll refer to your collection of work samples as the "portfolio."

Strictly speaking, a portfolio is an interview tool, an attractive package of written documents, photographs, slides, tapes, sketches and projects that reflect your best efforts.

Who Needs A Portfolio?

If you are trying to sell yourself as a communicator or a visual artist, you will need to show an up-to-date portfolio when you seek your first job in the field, when you change jobs and, sometimes, when you are up for a performance evaluation with a current employer. Should you decide to become a freelancer or consultant, you will need to show your portfolio to win new clients.

An effective portfolio presents evidence that you can relay a message verbally or visually, or both, to a third party. The portfolio is a sales kit for the most important product you will ever have to sell—yourself.

Who needs a portfolio?

Anyone preparing for a career in visual arts or in the communications field. And *that* means a lot more specific job titles than you might think.

Following are just some of the careers in which a portfolio is a valuable and necessary interview tool:

advertising copy writer
animator
broadcast copy writer
business communicator
camera operator
cartoonist
comp artist
correspondent
creative director
editor
editorial artist
electronic computer
    designer
fashion designer
fashion illustrator
floral designer
graphic designer
illustrator
industrial designer
interior designer
journalist
mechanical boardperson
medical and scientific
    illustrator

merchandise displayer
package designer
painter
photo illustrator
photo journalist
promotions manager
public relations specialist
publicity writer
radio announcer
reporter
screenwriter
sculptor
sketch artist
stage and set designer
stylist
teacher
technical illustrator
technical writer
television writer
television announcer
textile designer
theatrical costumer
video producer
writer

What To Include In Your Portfolio

You should include samples of your expertise that reflect your professional abilities and communicate to a potential employer the fine work you're capable of doing.

An effective portfolio is *not* a static package of your work. There is no single arrangement of work samples that will be suited for all the job interviews you will go through. So you must collect as many good samples as you can and be prepared to select and rearrange samples in preparation for each new interview according to each employer's needs.

What form your work samples take will depend on your academic training and your own particular area of expertise. Not all writers, for example, are proficient in the same kinds of writing.

A journalist's portfolio might contain news stories, feature stories, an editing sample and an obituary. The portfolio for a public relations writer, on the other hand, might hold a news release, a grant proposal, newsletter copy, and the layout and design for a brochure.

Even though both writers' portfolios contain typed copy, the formats and styles of writing vary considerably.

In the visual arts occupations, portfolios will differ according to the medium and specialty of the artist, designer or photographer.

Some photographers, for example, develop expertise with certain camera techniques or films; others specialize in photographing certain subject matter. A photographer's portfolio could be a tray of slides. It might be an attache case filled with mounted black-and-white prints. Or a binder filled with tear sheets of the photographer's published photos.

The portfolio of a video camera operator might consist of a single video cassette on which he or she has included several examples of his or her best work.

Designers and visual artists usually specialize in one type of product or activity. For example, a fashion designer might develop an expertise in designing knitted fabrics and garments. His portfolio might contain fabric samples, knit graphs and sketches for sweater designs.

An illustrator, on the other hand, might develop a specialty in drawing people or animals. Her portfolio might contain pen-and-ink sketches as well as watercolor illustrations suitable for publication in a medical textbook.

If you are a student, or you're reentering the job market in a new field, you may not have many professional samples to include in your portfolio. It's never too early to begin building your portfolio. And you'd be surprised at the creative opportunities you have to develop work samples that will enhance your portfolio.

You can begin to build a professional-looking portfolio that includes classroom assignments and extracurricular work. Chapter Two explains how you can draw from college work as well as volunteer activities to generate portfolio samples.

Chapter Three offers tips on how you can gain freelance experience.

And Chapter Four offers further suggestions on creating pieces that beef up your portfolio and help you land a job in the career of your dreams.

Where The Jobs Are

First, you'll need to find out about job opportunities. You can find out about possible employment from the following sources:

- *Want ads in the classified section* of the newspaper, especially the fat Sunday editions. If you can relocate, subscribe to the newspapers of cities in which you'd like to live.

- *Want ads in trade magazines and professional journals.* Some of these publications also run position-wanted ads in which you can list your job skills. (See pp. 23 - 24 for an example.)

- *Professional organizations* (see Appendix A for a partial list). Some groups have structured job networks, resume exchanges, job hot lines, etc. Informal contact with members can also yield job information.

- *College placement office.* Many companies send recruiters who interview job applicants right on the campus; other companies send printed information about current job openings. The placement office is the clearinghouse and distributor of this information.

- *Friends, relatives and acquaintances.* Make a list of any contacts who are working in your field or who work for a company that hires people with your qualifications. Call them and let them know that you're looking for work.

- *College instructors or academic advisers.* Sometimes employers will call professors and ask them to recommend individuals for certain entry-level positions. Ask your instructors to keep you in mind and to pass on any employment information that they receive.

- *Employment agencies.* Some charge a fee, so read your contract carefully. In some larger metropolitan areas, you may be able to locate an employment agency that specializes in placing people with your job skills—even if you're a "first-timer."

- *Trade shows, professional conferences and job fairs.* These group gatherings can provide you with information about your career field, and contacts that may lead to job offers.

When And How To Show Off

When you apply for a position, you will need to let the employer know that you have a portfolio.

Many students and beginners in the field won't have portfolios at all.

The fact that you have prepared one shows that you are *not* a novice—despite your possible inexperience—and that you are serious about getting the job.

You will want to let each employer know that you have a portfolio by referring to it in the resume and the cover letter:

- *In the resume:* The last line should read "Portfolio available."

- *In the cover letter:* Introduce the idea of an interview at which you could show your work.

In the business of marketing yourself, think of the resume and cover letter as advertisements for your skills. Include whatever information you believe will create interest in you. You might begin by consulting *Your First Resume* by Ron Fry or *The Resume Solution* by Dave Swanson, the first an excellent source for neophytes, the latter for more experienced professionals.

Some employers ask applicants to send work samples with the resume and cover letter. If the samples are good, then the employer will invite the applicants to show their portfolios.

Most employers of newspaper reporters, for example, will expect to see clips of published writing as a part of this initial screening of applicants.

How do you know whether to send such work samples with your resume and cover letter when you apply for a job?

Here are some guidelines:

- Send samples when an employer asks for them or the want ad for the job specifies that samples are expected.

- If you have any special experience that you think will fill an employer's job needs, send a sample that proves it.

Some counselors recommend that communications job seekers should always send work samples when applying.

For writers, this is easy advice to follow. Select a couple of your best clips, make copies, and send them out with your initial application package.

If your specialty is photography, broadcast or audio/visual production, however, sending out samples with every resume can become expensive. But if you think that your samples can give you an edge over competition for the job, the expense is worth it.

Advertise Yourself

Just as employers use the classifieds to advertise for employees, *you* can advertise your skills to potential employers. Trade journals and professional organization publications will often run advertisements for job seekers. (See Appendix A for a partial list of professional organizations for communications and visual arts professionals.)

Here is a typical position-wanted ad from an issue of *The Professional Communicator*, the journal of Women in Communications, Inc:

> Recent PR grad served as public-relations/marketing intern for commercial company. Experience includes desktop publishing, writing, developing ad copy, editing, layout/

design of newsletter and other company publications, and photography. Seeks position in
PR/Marketing in the greater Chicago area.
Portfolio available. Contact Jill Student, 2112
13th Street, Glenview, IL 60025; (312)296-0000.

Chapter 2

Just For Students

Turning Non-Professional Experience Into Professional Portfolio Materials

A solid selection of professional-looking work samples is paramount in proving to a potential employer that you have the expertise to do the job.

Yet if you're a student, or just entering the field, you may not have a lot of experience to select from.

You can, however, maximize your student or non-professional experiences and add plenty of powerful, job-winning work samples to your portfolio.

Turn your college experiences into materials for your portfolio.

There are a number of actions that you can take while you are still in school to help you build a professional-looking portfolio.

If you don't take advantage of at least a few of these opportunities, you may have a tough time later in competing for jobs.

Don't wait until your senior year to look into these suggestions. It will already be much too late!

Turning Classwork Into
Portfolio Material

Depending on where you are attending college, your required courses will be determined by your major. You and your adviser will determine early in your college experience just what courses you must take.

In addition to your required courses, you will probably have an opportunity to select electives from outside your department. Don't be afraid to explore courses that are not in your specialty area.

For example, the ***Occupational Outlook Handbook*** suggests that courses in political science, computer science, psychology and marketing are useful for someone interested in a career in public relations.

Classes in math, physics and chemistry are useful for photographers who need to grasp the workings of lenses, films, light sources and developing processes.

Courses in writing are useful for graphic artists who will be working with writers as part of a creative team.

If there are no courses offered that suit your special interests, you may be able to conduct independent study for which you receive college credit. Ask your academic adviser about your options.

Whatever courses you choose, be sure to consider these portfolio-building opportunities:

- Check with your instructors to see if any of the assignments you will have to complete will be suitable for your portfolio. (See Appendix B for an especially useful assignment.)

- Sign up for production courses that require you to complete a major project by semester's end.

- If you take writing courses, try to get your writing published in the campus paper or magazine.

- If you take photography or art & design courses, save copies of all completed assignments.

"But I can't put a class assignment into my portfolio," you may be thinking. *You certainly can, and you must.*

When you apply for your first communications job, employers won't expect you to have a lot of published or produced samples. If your resume indicates that you spent the past few years in the classroom, you should anticipate that employers will want to see samples of techniques that you learned as a student.

In a portfolio development class he teaches at Kent State University's Department of Art, Professor John Buchanan tells students to include their sketchbooks in their portfolios.

"A sketchbook shows a single project from initial inception through to the production stage," says Buchanan. "Employers looking at student sketchbooks are interested in the decision process: What made the individual reject one idea and use another? That decision process can give clues as to what kind of an employee the student will become."

If you are applying for a writing job, it's a good idea to include a sample of unpublished writing even if you have several published articles. Beverly Pierce, Manager of Public Relations at the BF Goodrich Company, told a group of students that she insists on seeing samples of unedited, unpublished writing from applicants who apply for writing positions in her department.

Dale Allen, Senior Vice President and Editor of the *Akron Beacon Journal,* asks job applicants to include a 750-word essay on an assigned topic as part of the portfolio package.

In both instances, these employers are looking for examples of *original* writing from job applicants.

A sample of unpublished copy, such as a class assignment, shows a prospective employer how much time and effort it will take to make that writer's work suitable for publication. So even if you are a writer with many published articles, by all means, include at least one example of raw (unpublished) copy in your portfolio.

If it's a class assignment, make sure that it is typed and proofread.

Don't include papers with the grade and teacher's comments scribbled in the margins. If you do, you may find that the interviewer is more curious about comparing opinions with the teacher than reviewing the quality of your work.

Join The Club

Extracurricular activities of any kind can help you to become a well-rounded individual. Unfortunately, not all of the activities you participate in during your college years translate into resume or portfolio material.

Try to get involved with as many media-related extracurricular activities as time permits in order to increase your chances of getting your work published or produced. Typical on-campus media opportunities include the student newspaper, yearbook, literary journals and magazines, college radio stations and television stations.

Internships

An internship experience offers you an opportunity to sharpen your skills in a work setting rather than in the classroom. Usually, student interns receive college credit for their work just as they would receive for classwork. More often than not, the intern is paid by the company for which he or she is working. In addition to work experience and future business contacts, an internship offers further opportunities to develop professional portfolio materials.

In most cases, internships are awarded on the basis of a student's grades, ability and advanced level of study in a particular area. Internships may be awarded within your academic department or you may apply for an internship directly. For lists of internship opportunities, be sure to consult the following sources:

- *Internships, Vol. 1: Advertising, Marketing, Public Relations & Sales*, Ron Fry, editor, The Career Press.

- *Internships, Vol. 2: Newspapers, Magazines and Book Publishing*, Ron Fry, editor, Career Press.

- *Internships, Vol. 5: Radio & Television Broadcasting & Production*, Ron Fry, editor, The Career Press.

- *Internships*, Katherine Jobst, editor, Peterson's Guides.

Cooperative Education Programs

If you want experience and a paycheck from working in a career field before you graduate, you may choose to take advantage of a Cooperative Education, or Co-op program. Through Co-op, you are placed in a paying position in the work force, with alternate semesters or terms in the classroom. The majority of the Co-op programs also award academic credit for the work experience. In 1988, more than 1,000 schools placed students in Co-op positions with nearly 80,000 employers across the country, according to the *Occupational Outlook Quarterly* (Fall, 1988).

Co-op allows you to experience a career field while you are still in school. In addition to the opportunities for developing portfolio samples, the experience may lead directly to a job once you graduate. The National Commission on Co-op Education reports that 40 percent of Co-op students continue working for their Co-op employers after they graduate and another 40 percent find jobs in fields related to their Co-op job. If you are interested in Cooperative Education, you should check with your college Co-op office, placement office or career center.

Work-Study

Nearly all colleges and universities offer some type of financial aid through work-study programs at which students work part of the day or week at an on-campus location. If you qualify for this type of experience, your college may try to place you in a job in which you can use your skills. The practical experience you get from a work-study program can help you build your portfolio and advance your professional prospects as well.

Getting Involved In Your Profession

An opportunity to develop portfolio materials is one of the benefits of joining a professional organization while you are still a student. Typically, an organization such as Women in Communication, Inc., will sponsor a student chapter. Student members conduct their own meetings and programs, and they may also be invited to attend the professional chapter's meetings for free or at a reduced cost.

In addition to meeting seasoned professionals and making important contacts, students enjoy opportunities to work on career-related projects or programs—experience that may add quality work samples to their portfolios!

Appendix A offers a partial listing of professional organizations for workers in communications and visual arts occupations. For a more complete listing, consult *The*

Encyclopedia of Associations, a reference work which should be available in your school or local library.

To find out if your college has student chapters of these organizations, check with the office that oversees student development on your campus.

Charity Begins At Home

Turn your volunteer work into materials for your portfolio.

You can contribute to a cause that's close to your heart, or participate in a social organization that you enjoy—*and* build your portfolio! Social service agencies welcome volunteers, especially those with special skills. If you're not already involved with a volunteer group, it's easy to contact one to offer your services.

If you are already involved in volunteer activities, you can use your experiences to build up your portfolio while you help others through service to your community. For example, one volunteer for a drug hot-line designed the descriptive literature for the service. In another instance, a PTA member volunteered to be the class historian at her son's elementary school, and photographed all the school's social events during the year. Both of these individuals included in their portfolios work generated by their volunteer activities.

Think about all the time you donate to community service projects. How much of that time is spent in using the very same skills you are trying to market to an employer? Just because you didn't get paid for the work doesn't mean that you can't include it in your portfolio.

Additionally, many employers value community involvement in their employees. By including portfolio samples that exhibit your volunteer activities, your potential employers learn that you are an involved, concerned individual.

Chapter 3

Getting Your Work Published

And Including It In Your Impressive Portfolio

Unfair as it may seem, given a group of otherwise similarly qualified communications or visual arts job seekers, the applicant whose portfolio contains published work is more likely to impress an employer. And, therefore, more likely to land an interview, more likely to get offered the job.

One way to get your work published *and* get some paid job experience, whether you are still in college or currently working, is to freelance.

Freelancers are professionals who take on specific assignments from clients for a fee. They may make a living from these assignments or freelance to supplement other sources of income.

The Catch-22 for you, the would-be freelancer, is that many companies you approach for assignments will want to see a well-developed portfolio—chockfull of previously published freelance assignments—before they'll feel comfortable giving you your *first* freelance assignment.

Sound a little like the entry-level job that requires two years experience? It should. But students lacking any experience *do* land such jobs. *You* can land an assignment.

The Odds Against You

If you are a photographer, artist or a designer, breaking into freelancing can be tough because so many professionals in the field are self-employed. *According to the U.S. Department of Labor, almost two-thirds of all visual artists were self-employed in 1986; about half of all photographers and camera operators were self-employed.*

In other words, landing a freelance assignment may well require you to compete—and beat out—a number of already established professionals.

Nevertheless, if you've got the talent and the desire, you *can* succeed. How do you make contact with businesses that hire freelancers? These steps will get you started:

- Draw up a list of people you know who work in the field—relatives, friends, acquaintances and colleagues. Include on the list anyone you know who already uses freelancers or who might be persuaded to try the services of a freelancer.

- Have some business cards printed listing your skills and services. If you have the ability, write and design a self-promotional brochure as well.

- Contact by letter the names on your source list; tell them about your skills and your wish to take on freelance assignments. Refer to the well-written query letter on p. 43. Include a business card, a brochure or a sample of your work, if feasible. Follow up with a phone call asking for an assignment.

- Be sure your portfolio is ready in case a client wants to see more of your work before giving you a job.

- Don't disregard your professors as potential sources of freelance contacts. Employers without established lists of tried-and-tested freelancers will often contact universities seeking competent students for short-term projects.

If you are trying to build your portfolio through freelance assignments, leave a business card with each of your professors. Let them know what kinds of skills you have and what jobs you are willing to do. You may find that these professors will continue to refer clients to you long after you graduate.

Count on spending a good deal of time marketing yourself just to land a freelance assignment. But if you do a good job on your first assignment, you may eventually end up with more freelance work than you imagined.

Don't underestimate the quality of persistence when you are trying to break into freelancing. One student achieved overwhelming success in landing freelance writing assignments. Her secret? She offered to do the first assignment for each client *for no charge*. Those clients who took advantage of her offer and liked her work remembered her the next time they needed a writer.

Breaking Into Print

If you are a photographer, consult the most recent edition of the ***Photographer's Market*** (Writer's Digest Books) for a list of national markets for photographs. The 1989 edition, for example, lists more than 2,500 photo buyers, including advertising and public relations firms; audiovisual, film and video firms; book publishers; businesses and organizations; galleries; newspapers and newsletters; paper products; publications; record companies; and stock photo agencies.

This excellent reference book also gives advice on how to market and sell your photographs to these potential clients.

If you are an artist or designer, check out the latest edition of the ***Artist's Market*** (Writer's Digest Books), which contains listings of firms and publications that use freelancers. Each listing includes the company's artistic needs, names of contacts, how to make the first contact and tips for getting a freelance assignment.

If you are a writer (and maybe even if you're not) you will want to enhance your portfolio by including as many published articles as you can get. A published byline (your name in print as the author) is evidence that you have credibility as a writer.

If you're primarily a photographer or a graphic artist, you can maximize your chances of selling your work in the freelance market by writing stories to accompany your visual work. According to the ***Photographer's Market***, there are hundreds of markets looking for word/picture packages. Check the listings in that publication to discover who's looking for what.

For Writers Only

Some journalists begin their writing careers by "stringing" for a newspaper. A *stringer* is a reporter who covers the news in a specific city or region for a newspaper located in another city. The stringer writes the story or, more often, calls the information in to another writer on the newspaper staff. If this type of freelance writing interests you, contact the managing editors of several metropolitan newspapers for more information on opportunities. Keep in mind that the assignments you will get as a stringer will probably be routine "cover-the-meeting-in-200-words-or-less" stories—the meatier assignments are saved for the staff writers.

One of the best ways for a writer to get published is to freelance an article for a magazine. Although it is difficult for a novice to get published in many of the high-paying national publications (there are exceptions, so keep trying anyway), there are hundreds of smaller publications that rely on freelance contributions for much of their editorial content. These publications pay anywhere from several cents per word to several hundred dollars for a completed article.

The following five steps will help you to break into magazine freelancing:

---

1. Generate An Article Idea

Look into your own experiences for article ideas. For example, one communication student's experiences in searching for a job led her to write an article called "Job-Search Journal" for publication in a professional trade magazine.

Another student wrote a first-person account of his vacation experience in panning for gold. He sold the piece to a magazine for readers who enjoy outdoor recreation.

Perhaps you're a student who has had to research a number of topics for class papers, projects and presentations. Would some rewriting and updating turn any of that research into a feature article?

You might be a mother who has recently returned to the working world. Your research and efforts to find quality child care for your infant may result in an article idea for a local magazine, even for a national parenting publication.

Your personal and professional experiences provide a limitless source of article ideas. Other ideas may occur to you as you browse through magazines, newspapers, brochures, publicity releases, even the back of your breakfast cereal box.

When you find an idea that piques your interest, you have found the subject for a feature article.

2. Find Potential Markets

One valuable reference for writers looking for book and magazine publishers is the ***Writer's Market*** (also Writer's Digest Books). This reference is useful because it categorizes by subject matter both consumer magazines (publications you receive by subscription or buy at the newsstand) and business and trade journals (publications sent to readers in specific industries and occupations). Another reference source for freelance writers is ***The Writer's Handbook*** (The Writer, Inc.).

Read carefully the listings in both reference works to find those publications that might be receptive to your ideas. The listings include editorial guidelines and may list possible feature ideas as well. You'll also find the address, phone number, names of editors, payment terms, and tips for breaking into print at each publication.

Obtain copies of the magazines that offer the best marketing possibilities, and carefully study each issue in order to determine how to propose your idea to the editors.

In their book ***Free-lancer and Staff Writer*** (Wadsworth Publishing Co., 1986), William Rivers and Alison Work suggest that writers can gain a great deal of information about how to write articles for certain magazines by examining the following:

- ***Cover.*** What identity is the magazine trying to establish? How do the cover lines lure readers inside the pages?

- ***Masthead.*** What is the staff size? If staff is small, there's a good chance the editors rely on freelance articles.

- ***Table of Contents.*** If the authorship of the articles changes from issue to issue, the magazine probably uses freelancers. Check for any regular departments that appear monthly—are they open to freelancers?

- *Advertisements.* What are the demographics of the people who appear in the ads (age, gender, socio-economic level, etc.)? The people depicted in the ads will resemble the readers of the magazine in these factors.

- *Articles.* Study the length, tone and type of article the magazine runs. Look for clues on how to write for that publication—vocabulary level, expertise of the writers, etc.

- *Graphics.* Is the magazine in color? Are illustrations included for each article? What kind? Who provides the photos? Sometimes, acceptance of an article will depend on whether the writer can supply the necessary graphics.

Make a list of all the possible markets for your article idea based on your analysis of the *Writer's Market* or *The Writer's Handbook* entries and the copies of the magazines. Don't overlook the business and trade journals as potential markets for your writing and photography. These publications can be a good place for beginners as well as established freelance writers to publish their work. The *Writer's Market* lists more than 500 of these magazines, and the *Standard Rate and Data Service—Business Publications* edition lists an additional 4,500 or so more.

---

3. Do Preliminary Research

Before you approach an editor with your idea, you must be very sure that you can get the information you need to write the story if you actually get the assignment. You don't need to have written the story before you contact an editor, but you should first assess the available information on your topic and arrange at least one interview with an expert. A personal interview, or primary research, ensures that you are not merely planning to rewrite information that is already in print. The credibility and expertise of your interview source, in many instances, will determine the quality of your story idea and will determine whether you get the writing assignment.

4. Query The Editor

To avoid researching and writing an article that may be rejected, you will first want to query the editor of the publication you have chosen by writing a letter that outlines your story idea. Most editors prefer to see query letters rather than finished manuscripts at this stage. *The Writer's Market* will tell you which editors prefer that you send completed work.

A good query letter, such as the one presented on p. 44, should answer the following questions:

- What is your central idea?
- How will you research your topic?
- How do you plan to develop the idea in your article?
- What are your qualifications for writing the story?
- Can you provide graphics?
- When can you deliver the completed article?

If you have already published anything, send a copy of that work with the query letter. A published clip indicates that you are a professional, and it gets your accompanying query out of the slush pile of throw-away mail that editors receive daily.

Always send a self-addressed stamped envelope (SASE) with your queries.

If you haven't published anything yet, you should offer to write the article "on spec" (on speculation)," which means that you are willing to research and write the story without any promise of payment or publication from the editor. If you are a novice and offer to work on spec, an editor may be more willing to give you a chance.

If the response to your query is "yes," the editor will give you some direction and a firm deadline for the article. If the answer is "no," query the next publication on your list of potential markets, modifying your idea to suit the readers of that particular publication.

Unless an editor specifies that he or she is willing to consider "simultaneous submissions"—the same article idea sent to a number of publications at the same time—don't query more than one editor at a time. Magazine features, unlike straight news stories, are considered exclusives. So don't submit multiple queries, even though you may be tempted to do so in order to hurry along the process of marketing your writing.

5. Write The Article

When you get an assignment from an editor, make every effort to follow through with all that you promised in your query letter. Deadlines are important too, and if you encounter problems with your research or ability to follow through, be sure to inform the editor promptly.

Good Reasons To Freelance

Freelancing is an excellent way to generate samples to build up a portfolio.

Freelancing also gives you an opportunity to make professional contacts with employers who may want to hire you later as a permanent employee.

Finally, freelancing gives you an opportunity to demonstrate that you are dependable and reliable.

Every communicator and visual artist should be able to list at least one freelance experience on his or her resume.

Sample Assignment Query Letter

John Sloan

25 Center Court, Easton, PA 16917 (215) 555-5555

June 19, 1991

Andrew Timmons, Owner
Quick Print Services Shop
12 Main Street
Easton, PA 16917

Dear Mr. Timmons:

Do you or your customers ever wish you had a writer on staff to help with the wording of printed pieces? The next time you or your customers need writing help, I hope you'll call on me.

I can help you with writing, editing and proofreading any of your printed pieces, including:

Ad copy	Fliers
Brochures	Instruction sheets
Bulletins	Letters
Catalogs	Order forms

I am enclosing some of my business cards, which I hope you will distribute to your customers who may need my help. Next week I'll call you to see how I might be able to help you with your business-related writing, editing and proofreading needs. If you need to call me, I can be reached at the phone number printed on my card.

Sincerely,

John Sloan
Freelance writer

enc.

Sample Article Query Letter

ALEXIA ANDREWS
25 Spicer Hall
The University of Akron
Akron, OH 44325

July 14, 1991

Ms. Ann Sheldon Mezger
Beacon Magazine
44 E. Exchange Street
Akron, OH   44328

Dear Ms. Mezger:

If The University of Akron campus seems eerie and haunted at night, it may be because the spirits once laid to rest there have returned for a visit.

Most of the students and faculty don't know that their campus was once the resting place (but not the *final* one, as it turned out) of the founding families of Akron. Many of those bodies were buried where Buchtel Hall now sits. But in 1870 the bodies were moved across town to Glendale Cemetery.

Would your readers be interested in a 1,000-word feature about what happened on "moving day"? According to my research at the University archives, some bizarre incidents took place when the bodies were removed. For example, one cemetery resident had a coffin fitted with a glass window. When the coffin was unearthed, witnesses were greeted with a view of Miner Spicer's perfectly preserved face, 16 years after his death.

I plan to interview the University historian for more anecdotes, and obtain through him pictures of The University, 1870 vintage. I could complete my research and have the feature ready for you by Halloween. I am willing to undertake the assignment on speculation.

I am majoring in communications at The University of Akron. Last semester I wrote for the campus newspaper—I have enclosed a clip of one of my published articles.

I hope to hear that you are interested in my idea outlined in this letter. I have included a SASE for your reply.

Cordially,

Alexia Andrews

enc.

Chapter 4

Putting It All Together

Creating The "Book" That Will Sell Your Work...And You

Ideally, when selecting work samples for your portfolio, you should have as large a collection as possible from which to choose. Granted, that usually is not the case if you are seeking your first job in the communications or visual arts fields—most entry-level job seekers will have to create work samples to round out their portfolios.

But whether you're selecting from a plethora of already published samples or creating enough new ones to at least fill the book, you should be guided by two very important rules when putting your portfolio together: *Focus your portfolio* in order to highlight your communication specialty and *tailor your portfolio* to each employer *every time you prepare to interview.*

Focusing Your Portfolio

In the communications and visual arts fields, many professionals have a variety of skills. A newsletter editor has experience in writing, publication design and production. Advertising copywriters sometimes have to provide sketches in order to communicate a concept to a client. Photographers usually write their own captions or may need to provide copy for a photo essay.

Even if you have a multitude of skills, you should put together a portfolio that highlights your *specialty*. If you're seeking a career as a writer, include your writing samples but leave out even your award-winning photographs and designs. Unless you are certain that an employer is looking for a combination of skills, select work samples that focus the employer's attention on your particular expertise. Resist the urge to include anything that doesn't apply.

Be very critical when selecting samples to include in your portfolio. Your very best work can get watered down if it's sandwiched between mediocre pieces.

And always check, and re-check, your samples for accuracy and neatness. A typo in a writing sample or a sloppy mechanical can create a bad impression about your capabilities and your judgment (see pp. 62 & 64 for tips on proofreading). If there is even one error in your sample, leave it out. Your portfolio should create an impression that you are a competent, skilled professional ready to put your talents to work.

Tailoring Your Portfolio

Be prepared to change your portfolio for every interview by taking pieces out, adding or creating new ones, rearranging and prioritizing the contents *each time you interview with a different employer*. This way, you are customizing your portfolio to show that *your specific expertise* will fulfill *that employer's particular needs*.

Tailoring your portfolio requires that you research both the employer's company and the industry in general. Appendix C lists some library resources that can help you.

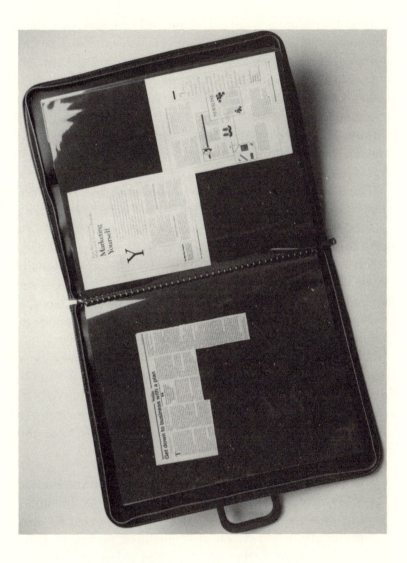

This writer purchased a large, 17 X 22 portfolio case so that she could display entire articles on a single page. The tear sheets are removable in case an interviewer wishes to make copies to distribute or read later.

In most cases, a want ad alone will not give you enough information about the job in order for you to determine which samples to include in your portfolio. Do that extra work—find out as much as possible about the company.

Let's say you're interviewing for a promotions copy-writer position with a large publishing company. Call the Human Resources department and ask for samples of existing promotional materials. Perhaps they may even have a job description for your position.

The more you can learn about the company, the job and what will be expected of you, the better you can prepare for your interview and select work samples that will reflect the skills that your interviewer is seeking.

Explore as many avenues of information as possible. Check with acquaintances who work at the company or in the industry. If you're a student, ask your professors, advisers or other students who may have had job experiences in that area—or even (lucky you!) with that company.

When you have completed your initial research, you may find that you don't have enough samples that you think will impress the prospective employer. You may need to create some. Here are three examples of industrious job applicants who developed work samples to enhance their portfolios for the job they were seeking:

- A graphic designer prepared for an employment interview at an automotive magazine by designing sample layouts for the feature pages of the publication. First, he studied back issues of the magazine, and then he designed a layout format for a new issue, pasting in pictures and copy he cut out of other publications. He set headlines by using press type that he purchased at an artist's supply store. His finished paste-up helped win him an entry-level job with the publication.

- An applicant for a public-relations position landed her job by writing and designing (using desktop

Portfolio pages come in an assortment of sizes and types. Here are four: The top sheet is an 8 1/2 X 11 page protector with black background sheet, punched to fit a three-ring binder; the second is an 8 1/2 X 11 clear page protector; the bottom sheets show two sizes of page protectors punched to fit a multi-ring binder.

publishing software) a sample newsletter for a robotics company. She included the piece when she submitted her resume and cover letter requesting an interview with the company. Before the interview, she wrote and designed a second issue of the newsletter and included it in her portfolio.

- A jewelry design student secured an internship by researching and designing a line of bracelets for a manufacturer of costume jewelry. Within the few days before her interview, she developed color sketches that were precise enough that a jeweler could use them to create models.

Creating customized work samples is an innovative way to tailor your portfolio to employers. But in some cases, this can cause problems. In her book, ***How to Put Your Book Together and Get a Job in Advertising*** (Hawthorn Books), Maxine Paetro cautions job applicants against creating ads for actual accounts of the advertising agencies they are approaching. For example, if you know a certain ad agency has an account with the XYZ Car Company, *don't* create an ad for that account to include in your portfolio. To avoid possible lawsuits, most agencies have a policy against reading unsolicited ideas for their clients' products.

What else should you avoid including in your portfolio? In his book, ***Graphic Design Career Guide***, James Craig advises that you leave out anything, such as political or religious materials, that could be considered controversial.

Your lighthearted, tongue-in-cheek article in the church bulletin might be misunderstood by your interviewer.

Or the attention-getting pamphlet you designed for a local political candidate might just draw the wrong kind of attention if that candidate proposes legislation that may be considered hurtful to your prospective company.

The multi-ring portfolio case has a zipper closure and pockets on the inside covers for bulky items and extra resumes. Flat items can be presented on the loose-leaf pages, protected by a nylon or acetate sleeve. These portfolio cases come in an assortment of sizes and colors.

If there is any possibility the sample could be offensive, or the intent could be misunderstood, eliminate it from your portfolio.

One final caution in choosing samples for your portfolio: If you plan to include a piece that you've just recently completed, or are still developing (including Co-op, internship or freelance projects), make sure that the project is neither sensitive nor confidential. Particularly if you are currently employed, you're not in a situation to ask your employer for permission to use the work.

So, when in doubt, leave it out.

Assembling Your Portfolio

What physical form your portfolio package takes will depend on the format, size and media of your work samples. You will want to present those samples in a way that shows off your skills and abilities. And your portfolio will have to be portable enough to carry with you from interview to interview.

Here are some suggestions for assembling your portfolio, followed by specific advice for writers, photographers, and designers and artists:

- Ask co-workers and other professionals or fellow students and professors to review your materials and suggest which pieces they believe are the best samples of your work.

- Avoid explanatory labels or titles, whether your portfolio contains photos, writing samples or design pieces. Remember, the portfolio is an interview tool. You will be there to offer additional explanation if your interviewer has any questions about your samples. For the most part, your work should speak for itself, and excessive detail should not be necessary for the interviewer to judge the

This photographer's portfolio contains images in a variety of formats, including a proof sheet and an enlargement of a selected shot. (Materials from the portfolio of Rick Zaidan.)

merits of your ability. If you feel that some written explanation must be included, here are three options:

1. Caption each page.

2. Insert titled divider pages to separate each sample or category of design included in your portfolio.

3. Include a short, typed description or explanation with the design, and position the paragraph where it won't distract the viewer from the design itself.

• If you believe you'll need to explain particular samples in more detail to your interviewer, prepare yourself with a brief explanation.

• Position all your work in the same direction, so that the interviewer doesn't have to turn the entire portfolio package around to view each image

Portfolio Tips For Writers

Most writers use a zippered multi-ring carrying case—which comes in 11" x 14", 14" x 17", 17" x 22" and 18" x 24" sizes—to show their samples.

If you specialize in writing features or have many large pieces of published copy, use the 17 x 22 portfolio. Otherwise, the 14 x 17 portfolio is a good size for displaying most of your writing samples, and you can have oversized articles reduced to fit the portfolio page.

The 11 x 14 size does not allow for an attractive arrangement of printed samples. And the 18 x 24 size is far too big to show off columns or pages of print, and it is bulky to carry and present for viewing.

A photographer's portfolio ready for mailing to an out-of-town employer is well-protected. Slides are inserted into a vinyl slide sheet, sandwiched between two pieces of cardboard, and then mailed along with a self-addressed stamped envelope (SASE).

A standard black three-ring binder is a good choice of portfolio case for business and technical writers who specialize in producing 8 1/2" x 11" typed documents (letters, memos, executive summaries, etc.). You can buy loose-leaf protector pages, with or without a colored background sheet, to fit the three-ring binder.

Zippered portfolio cases come with loose-leaf pages protected with acetate, vinyl or polyester coverings that allow you to slip documents against a black background page. You can buy extra pages at most office or artist supply retailers (or check your college bookstore). But because you will be carefully limiting your portfolio contents to your very best writing samples, the pages that come with the case will probably be enough to get you started.

Most portfolio cases will also have pockets on the covers. Bulky pieces, such as annual reports, computer disks, tapes and booklets, can be stored in these pockets, along with extra copies of your resume and any copies of work you want to leave behind after each interview.

Underneath the protector sheet, insert your tear sheets (whole pages from publications in which your articles appear) or clips (your article cut out of the page). If you don't have clean, original copies of your work, use high-quality photocopies of the original published samples. Use the center page spreads to display your longer pieces. If a single article still does not fit on a spread, you can have it reduced to fit or you can include only part of the original.

Include only one writing sample on a page, unless you have several very short items of the same kind (e.g., news releases or spot commercials) and you want to group them together on a single page to emphasize your experience in a given format. Make sure all the pieces are inserted facing in the same direction, so that the interviewer doesn't have to spin the binder around to read your clips.

Even though the writing samples may slip around a bit under the page protector, it is best *not* to mount them permanently onto the background page. One reason is that

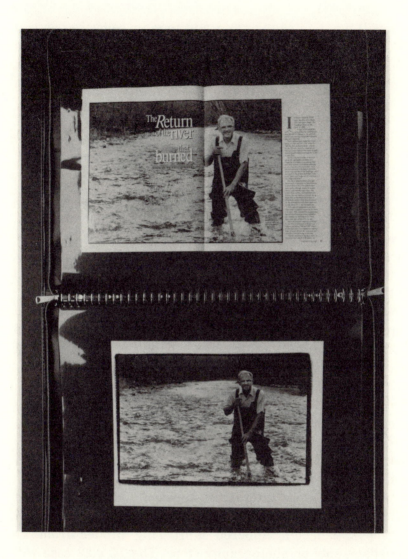

This photographer's portfolio displays a black-and-white enlargement and a tear sheet from the publication in which the photo was published. (Materials from the portfolio and courtesy of Rick Zaidan.)

you will want to change and add to your collection as you get more experience. If you don't mount your samples, this task is more easily accomplished. Another reason is that some employers may want to remove samples and have them copied to read after the interview.

Portfolio Tips For Photographers

A photographer's portfolio could be a tray of slides, a collection of mounted prints, a three-ring binder of contact sheets (sometimes called proof sheets, showing in miniature all the shots on an exposed roll of film), or even a book of tear sheets. It could also be a combination of some or all of these formats.

If you are preparing a portfolio to mail to out-of-town employers, the slide portfolio is the most inexpensive and convenient format. To prepare a slide portfolio, you will have to get slide copies of your prints, tear sheets and contact sheets. Mail the slide collection in plastic slide sheets. These sheets can be purchased at photography stores. Each sheet holds up to 20 35mm slides that can be viewed over a light table. Make sure your name, address and copyright notice (the © symbol, your name, the year) appear on each slide.

For face-to-face interviews, however, you can present your work in print and slide format in the same portfolio casebook. Select a zippered multi-ring binder from an artist's supply or photography store. The 17 x 22 case will accommodate photographs as large as 16 x 20. The case will include several removable pages covered with plastic or acetate, into which you can insert your prints, mounted or unmounted. Include tear sheets and contact sheets as well, one sample per portfolio page.

If you plan to include slides in your portfolio, insert them into plastic slide sheets and put the sheets into the pocket inside the portfolio case. If you wish, you can mount

These large color transparencies, mounted between two pieces of black mat board, are ready for viewing over a light table. (Transparencies from the portfolio of Rick Zaidan.)

your transparencies—individually or in selected groups—in black mat board cards that you either purchase or cut yourself. Store these cards in your portfolio pocket.

Some photographers and designers prefer to mount all their samples on mat board. This allows employers to focus on one piece at a time, and the mat board protects the work during handling. If you choose to mount your work in this way, you won't need the multi-ring binder. Instead, you may wish to purchase an attache case, sometimes called the "Madison Avenue style portfolio", to hold your work.

Select your samples carefully. Don't include any spotted or unfocused shots. Your work has to be flawless to withstand the scrutiny of the interviewer.

Portfolio Tips For Designers & Artists

Designers and artists usually present their work in a zippered multi-ring case. Some, however, prefer to mat, mount and/or laminate their work samples and carry them loose in an attache case. If you are a recent graduate looking for your first job, you will probably choose to organize your work samples in a multi-ringed case so that you can dictate the order in which you present your work to an interviewer.

Begin by measuring your largest work sample and select a case to fit it. The most popular size case for designers and artists is 14 x 17. If you have a few samples larger than this size, you can have your work photographed or reduced to fit the format. You can put bulky pieces into the pockets in the portfolio cover.

Arrange your samples in sequence for presentation (Chapter Five offers organization suggestions), inserting each sample underneath a page protector. Some designers and artists prefer to mount each piece of work against the background page so that they can permanently position the

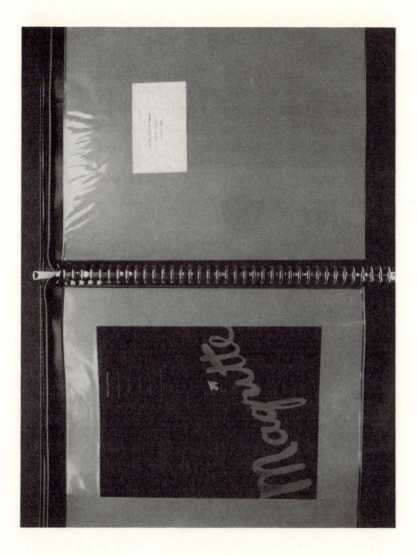

This graphic designer's portfolio includes a paragraph of description on the page facing each design. When presenting the portfolio in person, the designer removes the paragraph and explains everything the interviewer needs to know about each piece. (Poster from the portfolio of Bruce Morrill.)

samples. Other designers prefer to insert loose samples so that prospective employers can take the pieces out of the portfolio case for better viewing.

Most portfolio cases include several pages of black background paper covered by a clear protector film. Because so much student design work is done in black and white, some new graduates remove the black pages and substitute neutral color background pages in order to better display their work.

How Important Is A Typo?

Make sure your employment documents are flawless. A single mistake, whether in a resume, cover letter or portfolio sample, can hurt your chances of landing an employment interview.

According to a recent survey by Olsten Services, one-third of the Fortune 1000 executives queried said they would automatically bypass someone whose resume contained a typo.

Most word processing packages are now equipped with spelling checkers, which makes proofing easier. But you can't rely on your computer to pick up *every* error. Homonyms (words that sound the same but are spelled differently) are only one problem your spell checker may not be able to handle—your computer might consider "their" correct, even though you *meant* "there." Numbers create other proofreading problems for computers--your system simply won't know if you've used the correct digits. Many spelling programs can't tell the difference between "eight" and "Eight"—meaning capitalization must be double-checked.

So don't rely on your computer to proofread everything. Here are 10 tips for proofreading whatever you write:

1. Save the task of proofreading for the first thing in the morning when your mind is alert.

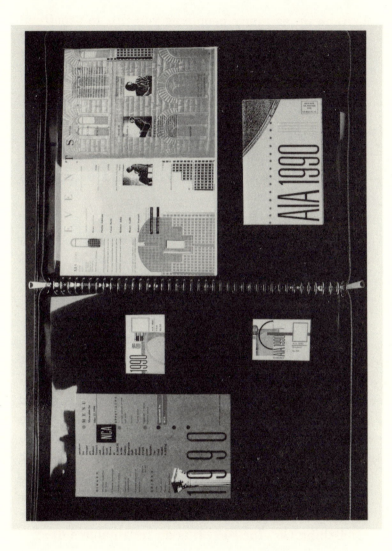

This graphic designer's portfolio displays several pieces from a single campaign. These pieces were created by a student for a class project, and although they were never printed, these samples showcase the designer's talent and skill. (Designs from the portfolio of Michelle Palko.)

2. Line up as many people as you can to proofread your copy. What you have written yourself is memorized, so you won't be as likely to spot errors as others will be.

3. If you must rely on yourself to proofread your own copy, don't proofread anything just after you have written it. Take a break and come back to it.

4. Proofread at least three times. You'll be surprised at how many errors you'll still find the third time around!

5. Don't proofread in one sitting.

6. Spelling errors in particular can be spotted more easily if you can separate words from the context of the copy. To do this, read your copy backward, from bottom to top.

7. Another way to proofread more thoroughly is to use an index card to uncover one word at a time.

8. Read the copy out loud to spot errors in context and meaning.

9. Keep a list of your most common spelling and usage errors next to your typewriter and refer to it as you proof.

10. Read a style manual at least once a year. A delightful, easy-to-read style book such as *The Elements of Style*, 3rd edition, by William Strunk, Jr. and E. B. White (Macmillan Publishing Co., Inc., 1979) is an invaluable aid.

Ten Tips For Preparing And Maintaining Your Portfolio

1. Keep your portfolio case looking spiffy on the outside: Polish it with shoe paste or spray-on furniture polish when the cover begins to dull.

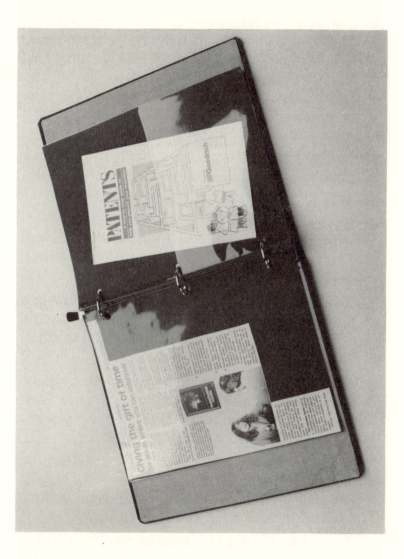

This writer's portfolio binder didn't have sewn-in pockets for loose items. The writer made a pocket by cutting away the top half of the protective acetate sheet that covered the loose-leaf page.

2. Fasten a luggage name tag to the front carrying handle of your portfolio case. The name tag not only provides identification, it also identifies the front of your case so that you can easily tell which way it opens. (Nothing looks worse to a prospective employer than fumbling with a portfolio; and if you can't even manage to *open* it smoothly, well...)

3. To reduce static cling on acetate-covered pages, wipe them with a fabric softener dryer sheet.

4. Most paper, including newsprint, can be pressed with a warm iron to remove wrinkles or creases. Dog-eared manuscripts can be made to look almost new.

5. The first page of your portfolio notebook will get the most wear and tear. Create a protector page out of heavy plastic or cardboard to cover the first page.

6. Wash your hands and dry them thoroughly before handling your work. Perspiration and body oils can permanently stain your papers, photos and other graphic materials.

7. Keep duplicates of all your work samples in a safe location other than your own home. If your original samples are stolen or destroyed by fire, you will be able to recreate your portfolio.

8. If your portfolio pages snag on the ring binder, modify the pages by enlarging the holes in the pages; or cut some of the holes away from the page so that only a few holes hold the pages in the binder.

9. Always keep extra supplies on hand (portfolio pages, materials for creating new work samples, etc.) so that you can make quick changes and/or repairs to your portfolio package.

10. If your portfolio case doesn't have pockets for loose samples, you can make one by cutting the top half off a page protector. Seal the bottom of the page protector with transparent tape and insert your clips, artwork, extra resumes, etc.

Chapter 5

Presenting Your Portfolio

Making It An Integral Part Of Your Interview

"Interview" is derived from the French *"entrevoir,"* meaning "to see" or "to glimpse." In that sense, interview is an especially appropriate term for job applicants who must prepare a portfolio to show to prospective employers. The portfolio allows the interviewer to see whatever skills and abilities the job seeker has chosen to display.

If your portfolio is *focused* on your specific talents and *tailored* to the employer with whom you will be interviewing, you have taken the first steps towards preparing for the all-important, face-to-face employment interview. But the success of the interview may depend as much on what you *say* about your work as what you *show*.

Although your portfolio may be the pivotal point around which the interview questions revolve, keep in mind that you should also be prepared to answer questions that are not necessarily related to your job skills. Such questions are designed to get you to reveal information about your character, your personality, and your general attitudes about work.

Be ready for them.

In the following section, I've reproduced a list of the questions most commonly asked at employment interviews. The list is updated periodically by the Placement Center of Northwestern University in Evanston, IL and published as part of the annual Lindquist/Endicott Survey.

These questions reflect a significant movement away from standard directive questions toward more open-ended situational queries. Common themes include applications of analytical, problem-solving and decision-making skills, leadership development, creativity, teamwork and personal development.

50 Most Commonly Asked Interview Questions

1. What goals have you set for yourself? How are you planning to achieve them?

2. Who or what has had the greatest influence on the development of your career interests?

3. What factors did you consider in choosing your major?

4. Why are you interested in our organization?

5. Tell me about yourself.

6. What two or three things are most important to you in a position?

7. What kind of work do you want to do?

8. Tell me about a project you initiated.

9. What are your expectations of your future employer?

10. What is your GPA? How do you feel about it? Does it reflect your ability?

11. How do you solve conflicts?

12. Tell me about how you perceive your strengths. Your weaknesses. How do you evaluate yourself?

13. What work experience has been the most valuable to you and why?

14. What was the most useful criticism you ever received, and who was it from?

15. Give an example of a problem you have solved and the process you used.

16. Describe the project or situation that best demonstrated your analytical skills.

17. What has been your greatest challenge?

18. Describe a situation where you had a conflict with another individual and how you dealt with it.

19. What were the biggest problems you have encountered in college? How have you handled them? What did you learn from them?

20. What are your team-player qualities? Give examples.

21. Describe your leadership style.

22. What interests or concerns you about the position or the company?

23. In a particular leadership role you had, what was the greatest challenge?

24. What idea have you developed and implemented that was particularly creative or innovative?

25. What characteristics do you think are important for this position?

26. How have your educational and work experiences prepared you for this position?

27. Take me through a project where you demonstrated _____ skills.

28. How do you think you have changed personally since you started college?

29. Tell me about a team project of which you are particularly proud, and your contribution.

30. How do you motivate people?

31. Why did you choose the extracurricular activities you did? What did you gain? What did you contribute?

32. What types of situations put you under pressure, and how do you deal with pressure?

33. Tell me about a difficult decision you have made.

34. Give an example of a situation in which you failed, and how you handled it.

35. Tell me about a situation when you had to persuade another person to your point of view.

36. What frustrates you the most?

37. Knowing what you know now about your college experience, would you make the same decisions?

38. What can you contribute to this company?

39. How would you react to having your credibility questioned?

40. What characteristics are most important in a good manager? How have you displayed one of these characteristics?

41. What challenges are you looking for in a position?

42. Are you willing to relocate or travel as part of your career?

43. What two or three accomplishments have given you the most satisfaction?

44. Describe a leadership role of yours and tell why you committed your time to it.

45. How are you conducting your job search, and how will you make your decision?

46. What is the most important lesson you have learned in or out of school?

47. Describe a situation where you had to work with someone who was difficult. How was the person difficult, and how did you handle it?

48. We are looking at a lot of great candidates; why are you the *best* person for this position?

49. How would your friends describe you? Your professors?

50. What else should I know about you?

Ask And Ye Shall Receive

Usually, an interviewer will give you an opportunity to ask questions as well. Your questions can reveal a great deal of information about your attitudes and values, so don't underestimate the importance of preparing some thoughtful questions to ask your prospective employer. If you are interested in the position, you should not leave the interview without asking questions like the following:

1. How does this company evaluate and promote employees?

2. What kind of training program is available for this position?

3. What is a typical career path at your company for someone starting in this position?

4. How is an employee in this position supervised?

5. How do my background and qualifications compare to other employees in similar positions within your company?

At this point in the interviewing process, you would be wise to avoid questions about salary, vacation days, lunch breaks and overtime and other benefit-related issues. If the interviewer is interested in you, there will be more than enough time to ask such details. But if you ask about them too early, you may hurt your chances to get hired at all.

Now, In The Center Ring

Guidelines for putting together an attractive physical package of your work samples were set forth in Chapter Four.

How do you prepare to *present* that wonderful package over which you've labored so long to an employer?

You may be asked to send in your portfolio for the employer to review before your interview or (more likely) to bring it with you. You could also be asked to leave it with the employer after the interview. In any case, if you are considered a serious candidate for the job, you will eventually have to answer questions about your work samples.

The arrangement and sequence of your portfolio contents should complement what you plan to say about each piece you included.

First, start with an empty portfolio case. Then, from your collection of work samples, select those that most closely match what you believe to be the requirements of the job (*focusing* the portfolio) and the employer's needs (*tailoring* the portfolio). Now, organize your selection of work samples in the order you want to talk about them.

Sharon Feodor screens dozens of applicants' portfolios a year in her position as personnel manager at Edgell Communications (Cleveland), a major publisher of business and trade journals. Her advice: Take special care in organizing your portfolio contents. Your organization scheme creates a lasting impression of your total ability as a communicator.

Organizing Your Portfolio

Although there are no rules to dictate the best way to organize your materials, you should give some thought to the overall impression you want to make. Here are a few different ways you can consider organizing your work:

- *By genre.* A journalist might organize his newspaper writing samples in sections such as investigative stories, meeting coverage, obituaries and feature stories. A designer's portfolio might include separate sections for book designs, book jackets, rough layouts and mechanicals.

- *From the simple to the complex.* A photographer's portfolio might be organized in black-and-white and color sections. A public relations writer's portfolio might begin with simple news releases and progress to full-length, fully researched feature articles.

- *For impact.* Start off with one of your best samples, follow with other pieces, end with another strong sample. Frequently, the last page of the portfolio will be left open on the interviewer's desk. Make sure your last page contains an impressive piece that leaves a positive impression about your work.

- *In chronological order.* This arrangement of your work shows your development throughout your training period. Use with caution, however, because this arrangement forces you to include your earliest work (and usually your weakest) in the portfolio.

- *By method of experience.* This method may work particularly well for students or recent graduates. You can organize sections for classwork, internship work, co-op work, freelance work, etc.

The technique you choose in organizing your portfolio contents should reflect the way you plan to talk about your work samples during the interview. You will need to practice what you want to say about your work. This planning is especially important for writers. The merit of a writing sample may not be apparent by merely looking at it. And an employer is not likely to take the time to read an entire piece while you sit there in silence.

When you assemble your pieces in the portfolio case, you should have all the pieces facing in the same direction. At the interview you will be presenting your portfolio on a desk or table top, and it is awkward for a viewer to have to turn the case in order to see the contents. Remove any blank pages in order to give the impression that the portfolio is full. If you have oversized pieces, or any samples that need to be unfolded or assembled, store them in the portfolio pockets and present them to the interviewer at the appropriate time—that is, when you have planned to talk about each in the sequence of presenting your work samples.

Playing Show & Tell

During the portfolio presentation, take the opportunity to bring up any special business or industry knowledge you may have gained, and point out any special problems you had to overcome in order to produce a sample. For example, deadlines are extremely important in the communications field. Did you produce any of your work under deadline pressure? Did you have to work with people outside your field in order to complete a project? Did you learn any new skills as the result of creating anything that you included in your portfolio?

Quite often, a printed piece is the result of a group effort. If you have any group projects in your portfolio, plan how you will describe your contribution to the piece. It's okay to include a group project in your portfolio as long as you tell your interviewer, and take only partial credit. Job applicants have a right to emphasize their strengths, but employers have a right to expect truthful information. Don't take credit for any aspect of a project that you weren't responsible for.

Here are a few examples of how some job applicants presented their work samples during employment interviews:

- An applicant for a public-relations job included in her portfolio a simple news release she had written to promote a club-sponsored event. The news release generated additional publicity in four of the five newspapers to which she mailed. At her employment interviews, the applicant was able to highlight her success with media contacts *and* show her writing ability.

- A student interviewing for a position at an ad agency included in his portfolio a copy of the *Standard Rate and Data Service (SRDS)* mechanical specifications with a quarter-page magazine ad he had created as a classroom assignment. *(SRDS* gives the circulation data, rates and mechanical requirements for most American print media.) By showing that he was aware of *SRDS* specifications and could design ads accordingly, the student presented evidence that he could make a successful transition from classroom assignments to advertising agency work.

- As part of a volunteer project, a photographer completed some work for a women's history television documentary. The pictures were incorporated into a historical series that was aired on public television and won a slew of awards. The producer of the series wrote a letter thanking the photographer for his part in the production.

When the photographer began his job search, he made sure to include the letter prominently in his portfolio of work samples.

• In her interview for a position as an assistant to a fashion designer, one job applicant explained how her research on fashion trends played a role in her sketches. She cited the sources of her information and explained how the information affected her design decisions. In this way, she demonstrated that she recognized the importance of keeping abreast of current fashion trends.

Through the interview experiences of these people, you can see how others have enhanced their portfolio contents with their commentary during the interview. Look at your own portfolio contents. What can you say about each of your samples that would impress an interviewer? Know your strengths, practice the points you want to make about your background and training, and by all means, emphasize the contributions you could make if you were hired.

After The Interview

A portfolio represents a substantial investment of your time and money, and you may feel reluctant to part company with your collection of work samples. But some employers will expect you to leave your work with them after the interview.

If an employer asks you to leave your portfolio, you should make every effort to comply. If the employer wants to see more of your work, it is probably because he or she considers you a serious candidate for the job. It might also mean that the final hiring decision belongs to someone else in the organization who must also screen your work. In either case, leaving your portfolio behind is virtually required to get the job.

Although some job seekers refuse to leave their portfolios, it certainly is wise for you to do so if you are truly interested in landing a job. Some job seekers purchase an extra case and fill it with duplicate work so that they are always prepared if an interviewer calls.

Most career counselors advise job seekers to write a brief letter or note after every interview, thanking the interviewer for the meeting and making reference to something that was discussed during the interview. This note also gives you an opportunity to present yet another work sample to those employers who have positions that interest you. (See p. 83 for a sample thank-you letter)

What should you send? If you have produced anything new since the interview, send it with the thank-you letter. If the interviewer expressed a special interest in any of your work, make a copy and send it. Finally, if the interviewer asked to see an example of work *not* represented in your portfolio, create it and send it with the thank-you letter. This gives you one more chance to get your name and work in front of the employer, and increases the likelihood that you will be remembered when the hiring decision is made.

Many job applicants go through a series of interviews with a single employer before they are finally hired, and then they may work for several weeks or months on a trial basis before they are considered official staff employees. Communications and visual arts are highly competitive fields, but if you have a professional-looking portfolio with good work samples, you'll increase your chances of getting the job you really want.

Keep Your Portfolio Updated

After you land that first coveted position, don't allow your portfolio to gather dust just because you finally have a job. I certainly don't mean to discourage you, but according to Richard Bolles, author of **What Color is Your Parachute?,** the average length of time an employee stays at the same job is only 3.6 years.

That doesn't mean 3.6 years from now you'd better start packing—an average doesn't mean *everybody*—but you can *certainly* expect to change jobs a few times in your working life. Which means more interviews. And an ongoing need to use your portfolio.

So no matter how satisfied you are with the job you've landed, how happy you are with your duties, how much you love your current boss, remember that nothing lasts forever and *keep your portfolio up to date* so that you can use it when it's time for a job change.

And note that Bolles' figure doesn't necessarily mean you will change *companies* every four years or so—3.6 years from now may be a great time to apply for and win that promotion to another department or to a more responsible job within your own. And your portfolio might well be a key ingredient helping you take advantage of such new opportunities *within your current company, too.)*

So document your on-the-job accomplishments and save copies of everything you do.

Seek out colleagues whose work you admire and ask them to review your portfolio. Edit accordingly, leaving out any samples that get a negative reaction. But don't expect your critics to agree—they may have definite, and conflicting, ideas. In the end, your portfolio should include what *you* consider to be your own best efforts.

A Look To The Future:
The Electronic Portfolio

Computers and electronic networks have changed society. Think about your own daily activities. Did you use a computer terminal at the library to help you find information for your assignment? Did you create your resume on a word processor? When you bought groceries, did the checkout clerk scan your purchases with a laser reader? Do you own a VCR, a CD player or a large-screen television?

Perhaps you already have pieces in your portfolio that were created using desktop publishing or computer graphics software. In the future, your entire portfolio may be assembled, stored, transmitted and received electronically. It's conceivable that a writer's portfolio could be stored on a single floppy disk. Artists' and photographers' portfolios could be stored on videocassettes.

How might such vast technological changes affect the job-seeking process itself? Instead of mailing or presenting your portfolio in person, you may be sending your work to potential employers electronically. Facsimile (FAX) equipment already allows you to convert printed images into electronic signals that can be sent over telephone lines to anyone with similar equipment.

External electronic mail systems transmit information through modems, devices that allow computers to "talk" over the phone. Instead of sending information on paper, correspondents merely type the receiver's phone number into the computer and send messages electronically. The information is received instantly.

The job seeker of the future may be interviewed by teleconferencing with potential employers all over the country. Teleconferencing allows parties in different locations the ability to communicate, without the high costs of food, lodging and transportation. An audio/video teleconference, for example, makes use of speakers to send sound, cameras to transmit video, and facsimile equipment to send printed information. Modern technology allows you, the job seeker, to sit in a specially equipped room in one part of the country and be interviewed (complete with portfolio presentation) by an employer in another part of the country.

A video portfolio? Your work samples on disk? A teleconference interview? The self-marketing opportunities available to you are indeed exciting! Yet, keep in mind that despite the advances in technology, nothing has been invented to replace *you*. When used to full advantage, the new technology is a merely a tool for your own creativity.

Try to keep up with the changes, but don't wring your hands over them. Use the new technology to help enhance your work, to make it easier.

But in the end, it is the quality of your ideas—your *thinking*—that will help you make your mark on the world.

Sample Post-Interview Thank-You Letter

Rudy LaSalle
25 Center Court, Easton, PA 16917 (215) 555-5555

June 21, 1989

Ms. Sareet Alzer, Creative Director
Anson & Anson Public Relations
43 High Street
Imperial, MO 63052

Dear Ms. Alzer:

Thank you very much for the opportunity to interview last week for the copywriter's position. It was a pleasure talking to you and learning more about Anson & Anson.

I want to reiterate that I am most interested in working for Anson & Anson. My degree in advertising/public relations and my experience writing copy for the university public relations department will enable me to become a productive member of your creative team.

In the interview, you talked about "pitch letters" as one type of writing required of Anson & Anson copy writers. Although I did not have an example of a pitch letter in my portfolio last week, I am enclosing a sample now to show you that I am able to write this type of document.

Thank you for your consideration. I look forward to hearing that you are interested in hiring me for the position of assistant copy writer.

Sincerely,

Rudy LaSalle

enclosure

Chapter 6

If They Could Do It...

Case Studies Of Successful
Portfolio Design And Presentation

In this chapter, you will meet five people who are preparing to enter the job market and one person who hopes to obtain an internship. These individuals are not real people, but their resumes, cover letters and portfolio contents are representative documents. These six case studies will give you some ideas and inspiration for assembling your own perfect portfolio.

Aiming For A Local Ad Agency

Benjamin Ellet is seeking a position as a graphic designer in an advertising agency. An industrious student, he has taken several courses that have allowed him to produce class projects. He is gaining career experience through an internship program. Additionally, he has taken on several freelance jobs for local businesses.

His job-search strategy is to send his resume and cover letter to every agency within driving distance of his home.

Although he will send copies of the same resume to every agency, he plans to customize his cover letters to individual employers. In the cover letter to Anderson Advertising Co. (see p. 87), Benjamin seeks to: (1) show that he is familiar with the firm by making reference to its new office; (2) show how his training and experience have prepared him for a career in advertising; and (3) create interest in his portfolio.

Benjamin's portfolio contains classroom projects and freelance work. Much of his internship work is incomplete (as well as confidential), so it cannot be included in his portfolio.

Here is a list of work that he *will* include in his portfolio:

- Sketch book in the pocket of the case. The book contains all the sketches for a single classroom assignment. The project is detailed from rough concept to final, comprehensive design. Benjamin is prepared to discuss why one design was chosen and the others discarded.
- Brochure designed for Ondrov Insurance Co.
- Tags and wrapping paper samples designed for a local flower shop.
- Menu and napkin showing calligraphy designed for Antwerp's Eatery; also, a photograph of the same design used as signage on the restaurant's delivery vehicle.
- Classroom project for advertising design class, including a series of magazine advertisements for a fictitious soft drink.
- Copies of fliers and forms created for a recent Ad Club conference.
- Letter of commendation for work performed as an intern, from the creative director at LMO Public Relations Co.

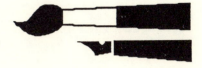

Benjamin Ellet
1830 Hildebrand Drive
Middleburg Heights, OH   44130

April 26, 199[0]

Kaye   Gunning
Creative Director
Anderson Advertising, Inc.
25 Euclid Avenue
Cleveland, OH   44325

Dear Kaye Gunning,

Experience, education, and enthusiasm. That's what I have to
offer as an employee of Anderson Advertising, Inc. Now that
you have opened an office in Cleveland, can you use a broadly
trained graphic design graduate who also has some practical
experience in the advertising field?

Please study my enclosed resume. You will see that my college
courses at Kent State University have given me a pretty good
foundation for a career in advertising. My student internship
and free lance experiences have shown me how to apply my
classroom knowledge to design projects for clients.

I would like to show you my portfolio, which contains examples
of my work on print advertisements, point-of-purchase displays,
and promotional pieces designed for my free lance clients.
You'll also see some ads I created in the classroom, represented
in developmental stages, from sketches to comps.

Next month, I will receive my B.F.A. in Graphic Arts and I would
like to begin my professional development with Anderson
Advertising , Inc. I will call your office next week to see
if you would be interested in setting up an interview so that
we can further discuss my qualifications for employment at your
firm.

Sincerely,

Benjamin Ellet

enclosure

Benjamin Ellet
1830 Hildebrand Drive
Middleburg Heights, OH   44130

Seeking a position as a graphic designer in an Advertising Agency

Education

Expect to graduate with a B.F.A. in Graphic Design from Kent State University, May 1990.

Design Work Experience

Graphic design intern, June 1989 to present, LMO Public Relations Co. Responsibilities include design, paste-up; emphasis on client and printer interaction, meeting deadlines.

Free lance designer, June 1987 to present. Clients include Ondrov Insurance Co., Ledbetter's Flower Shop, and Antwerp's Eatery.

Design Skills

Classroom training in design and layout, color theory, keylining, editorial and advertising illustration, calligraphy. Knowledge of computer graphics software applications.

Experience in design and production of advertising and publications promoting products and events for LMO Public Relations Co. clients.

Designed and produced posters, promotional materials, and registration forms for 1988 Ad Club conference.

Professional Memberships

Kent State University Ad Club (American Advertising Federation), 1987 to present.
Served as vice-president/membership,1988 academic year.

Public Relations Student Society of America, 1989 to present. Serve on publicity committee.

References and Portfolio available upon request

Seeking A Fashion Design Internship

Shana McWilliams is trying to secure an internship as assistant to a fashion designer in a knitwear company. She is a fashion design major at the Fashion Institute of Technology (F.I.T.). Shana's academic advisor made the initial contact with the internship supervisor at the knitwear company, who wants to see Shana's resume and portfolio before making any commitment to the internship.

During her three years at F.I.T., Shana has developed a library of sketches for her portfolio, and she has collected fabric swatches and yarn samples as well. For the internship portfolio presentation, she will present the following from her library of work samples:

- A collection of sweater designs using a nautical motif.
- A group of sketches showing cut-and-wear knit designs, including fabric swatches for some garments.
- A series of suit designs, including yarn samples.
- A line of sportswear designs for knitted garments.

Shana's portfolio will include almost 40 ideas, categorized in the four groups listed. She will show her designs as rendered plates, sketches done in markers. And, to show her understanding of production techniques, she will present her designs as "specs"—exact, technical drawings with dimensions that could be used for producing the garment. She also will show fabric swatches and yarn samples for her designs.

Her entire presentation will be organized in an 11 x 14 zippered, multi-ring binder. She will carry extra resumes with her to the interview (in the large pocket of the binder) in case she has to present her designs to others at the company.

RESUME

Shana McWilliams
888 Nutcracker Street
New York, New York 10035
(212) 922-2365

OBJECTIVE

Seeking an internship as assistant to fashion designer.

EDUCATION

Majoring in Fashion Design, Fashion Institute of Technology, New York. Expect to graduate with Bachelor's Degree of Fine Arts, June 1992.

DESIGN EXPERIENCE

While at F.I.T., successfully completed courses in Apparel Design, Flat Pattern Design, Textile Principles and Computer Graphics.

Tutored students in draping techniques during junior year at F.I.T.

WORK EXPERIENCE

Retail clerk, Macy's Department Store, summers of 1989 and 1990.

Receptionist for showroom, Allendon and Sons, Inc., New York, part time during high school.

ACTIVITIES

Member of the Apparel Design Association at F.I.T.

REFERENCES AND PORTFOLIO AVAILABLE

Moving From Computer Programmer To Writer

Thomas Paige has been working as a computer programmer for two years. One of his duties at his current job is to write technical training manuals for other employees who need computer instruction. Although his education and training are in computer applications, Thomas has found that he actually enjoys the writing part of his job more than working with computers.

A friend who works at the Allton Corporation told Thomas about an opening for a technical writer, the salary and benefits for which represent a definite step up the career ladder. In order to apply for this position, Thomas first has to create a portfolio of work samples. One problem: Many of the technical documents he writes on his current job are confidential and, therefore, cannot be included in the package.

Thomas Paige's portfolio is a three-ring binder that contains the following work samples:

- A resume.
- His college transcript.
- A computer graphics printout created to show how statistical data can be presented visually.
- The text to accompany and explain the graphics.
- Two writing samples created specifically for the interview at Allton.
- A (non-confidential) employee training manual created on the job.

Thomas is sending one of the writing samples along with his cover letter and resume. The friend who works at Allton gave him the name of the supervisor of technical writers, so Thomas will address his letter to that person rather than to the personnel director.

Thomas Paige
25 Oak Street
Building A, Apt. 3
Washington D.C. 20030

February 4, 1991

Ms. Elsie Madigan
Publications Department
The Allton Corporation
22 Boylston Avenue
Boston, MA 02857

Dear Ms. Madigan:

Margaret Pembroke, a systems analyst at your company, informed me about a possible job opening for a technical writer in your department. I hope you will review the enclosed resume and writing sample in order to evaluate me as a potential employee.

My education and work experience have provided me with:
- a rich background in writing
- strong technical experience
- skill in computer applications

The writing sample I have enclosed (data, text and graphic interpretation) will give you some idea of what I am capable of producing. I hope that we will be able to get together soon so that I can show you my portfolio of writing samples.

I will call your office next week to find out about any openings for technical writers, and to find out the next step in the application process.

Cordially,

Thomas Paige

Enclosure

Resume

Thomas Paige
25 Oak Street
Building A, Apt. 3
Washington D.C. 20030

Summary:

Several years of experience writing technical documents. Trained in computer applications necessary for interpreting data and translating data into text and graphics. Associate degree in computer technology, George Mason University. Graduated with honors, 1987.

Rich Background in Writing:

- Wrote 15 technical documents while employed as computer programmer at Hinden Company, including letters, memo report, training manuals, and proposals.

Strong Technical Experience:

- Studied two years of computer programming at college level.
- Skilled at computer applications, including spreadsheets, word processing, and graphics.

Highly Organized:

- Maintained a 3.4 GPA during college while working part time to pay expenses.

Very Dependable:

- Supervise six people for current employer.
- Commended by current supervisor for excellent work.

References and Portfolio available upon request.

Using Ads To Land A Job

Susan Weymouth is seeking a job as a photojournalist for a publication. Susan has placed position-wanted ads in a number of business and trade publications that are circulated to employers in the publishing industry. She has also placed similar ads in professional organization newsletters. Because these advertisements will circulate nationally, Susan is prepared to relocate in order to begin her career in photojournalism.

Susan's job-wanted ad reads as follows:

> Recent photojournalism grad with strong design background seeking position as a staff photographer/photojournalist. Experienced in using computer to design informational graphics. Familiar with a variety of camera formats and films. Experience working as staff photographer for a business weekly. Willing to work hard. Quick to learn new skills. Will relocate. Susan Weymouth, P.O. Box 142, Honolulu, HI 96837; 808/555-6776.

Susan's portfolio is a 16 x 20 multi-ring binder that contains the following:

- 8 x 10 black-and-white photographs from her internship at the weekly paper.

- Tear sheets from the issues of the weekly paper that contain her published photos.

- A slide sheet filled with 20 35mm color slides, contained in the portfolio pocket. Slides were from a class project.

- A series of three computer-generated informational graphics created during her internship at the weekly paper.

Because Susan expects to hear from out-of-town employers, she has also prepared a portfolio that can be mailed, which contains copies of the computer-generated graphics, copies of the tear sheets, slides of the black and white prints, and duplicates of the original color slides. All slides are marked with her name, address and copyright, and will be inserted into slide sheets.

The entire package will be sandwiched between two pieces of lightweight cardboard and mailed in a large manila envelope. Susan will also enclose a self-addressed, stamped envelope for the safe return of her portfolio.

(Her resume is reproduced on p. 96.)

Making The Blind See

Margaret West saw the following want ad in her local newspaper:

> Graphic Artist Wanted: Exciting opportunity in three-person art department at award-winning, monthly trade magazine. Requirements include strong design sense, creativity and organizational skills. Knowledge of computerized typesetting and desktop publishing helpful. Person must thrive on deadline pressure. Salary commensurate with experience. Send resume, two or three nonreturnable art samples and salary requirements to Box 36, c/o *Waterville Morning Sun*, 22 Hill St., Waterville, ME 04901.

Like many newspaper want ads, this one is "blind" in that it does not list the employer's name, address or phone number. Employers sometimes list ads this way so that they won't be deluged with unwanted telephone calls. The newspaper in which the ad was placed will forward all mail to the employer placing the ad.

Susan Weymouth

P.O. Box 142, Honolulu, HI 96837
808/555-6776

Job Objective

A position as a staff photographer/photojournalist.

Education

- B.A., Oregon State University, 1989.
- Degree in Photography, graduated with honors.

Skills

- Knowledgeable in the use of 35mm, 2 1/4 x 2 1/4, and 4 x 5 view camera formats.
- Knowledgeable in selection and uses of lenses and films; trained in both black-and-white and color photography.
- Trained in high contrast photography and experimental photography.

Work Experience

- 1988: Internship at *Corvallis Business Reporter*.
  Responsibilities included photographing events and people, production lab tasks, writing cutlines for photos and graphics, creating computer-generated graphics.
- Several photographs taken for *CBR* were picked up by national wire service.
- 1986-87: Work/study position in admissions office, Oregon State University.
  Responsibilities included typing, answering phone and creating computer-generated informational graphics for publication in recruiting literature.

Activities

- Member of Photography Club, Oregon State University, 1986-89; president, 1989.

Portfolio and references available upon request.

Margaret's portfolio will include the following work samples:

- Tear sheets of ads created for campus newspaper.
- Copy of a brochure she designed and helped write for a sorority event.
- Letter of commendation from her supervisor at J.C.Penney's.
- Sample publication mock-up she created for an interview with the art department of a monthly publication.

In her cover letter to the employer (see p. 98), Margaret discusses salary. For most entry-level positions, salary is fixed and non-negotiable, but in the want ad above the employer *asks* for salary requirements from applicants. Margaret studied **The Occupational Outlook Handbook** and similar reference works and talked to other designers to determine a general salary range for candidates with her qualifications working in her geographical area. She is prepared to name an annual salary figure, but is open to negotiation if the job offers good fringe benefits and good promise for career growth.

From Freelance To Full-Time

Adrian Wilis is looking for a full-time job in public relations after having been out of the job market for several years. During those years, Adrian freelanced several issues of a company newsletter and helped coordinate publicity for several events sponsored by the PTA. Recently, she completed a course in desktop publishing to upgrade her skills so she could re-enter the job market.

A friend told Adrian about a job opening for the editorship of a company newsletter, *ITR Today*. Adrian

Margaret West
21 Stillwater Ave.
Old Town, ME   04468

January 21, 1991

Box 36
c/o *Waterville Morning Sun*
22 Hill St.
Waterville, ME   04901

Subject: Graphic Artist Wanted Position

I am responding to your advertisement for a graphic artist, published in the January 20 issue of the *Waterville Morning Sun.*

Enclosed, you'll find my resume, which spells out my qualifications and accomplishments as a graphic design major at The University of Maine. I think that my experience on the campus publication has helped to prepare me for a career as a designer at a trade magazine. I enjoy the excitement of working under deadline pressure.

Regarding salary requirement: Because of my college degree in graphic design, I would expect to start at the upper end of the salary range for new employees at your company.

I hope that you will call me soon so that we can set up a meeting. I would like to show you my portfolio and talk to you more about my qualifications for the job. You can reach me most mornings at (207) 322-4567: My answering machine will take your message if I'm not home.

Cordially,

Margaret West

enc.

**IF YOU ARE LOOKING FOR AN EMPLOYEE WITH
A STRONG DESIGN SENSE,
CREATIVITY AND
ORGANIZATIONAL SKILLS,
YOU'LL WANT TO READ THIS:**

It's about a person named   **Margaret West**
21 Stillwater Ave.
Old Town, ME   04468
(207)322-4567

Education

She attended **The University of Maine** where she earned a **BA in Graphic Design** in 1988.

Special Skills

While she was a student, Margaret was a **Staff Designer for the campus newspaper.** She assisted with advertising design and page layout, using desktop publishing computer software.

Honors and Activities

She was also involved in other activities in college. During her senior year, Margaret **designed and helped write promotions literature** for the Tri Delta Special Lecture Series. She also helped to coordinate and schedule that series of twelve guest speakers.

She was chosen by portfolio to show her designs at the UM 1988 **Program of Editorial Design.**

Work Experience

To pay her college expenses, Margaret works part-time at J. C. Penney's in Bangor, where her supervisor commends her for her **dependability, enthusiasm and dedication.**

Now Margaret West is seeking a position as an **Editorial Graphic Designer.**

If you think she looks good on paper, you'll want to see her **Portfolio** and talk to her in person.

has researched the ITR Company, a mid-sized producer of polymer chemicals. She has also studied several recent issues of the newsletter, which contains information about employees, benefits, events and other company news. The publication also contains graphics; the masthead lists an artist on staff. The current editor is the only writer listed. Based on her analysis of the company and the newsletter issues, Adrian has created a portfolio to include the following work samples:

- Issues of newsletter freelanced for American Insurance Agency.

- Promotional materials from two PTA events she helped to coordinate and publicize, including a public service announcement for radio, a newsletter item for the local paper and a flier she wrote and designed by computer.

- Sample layout and copy for a single issue of *ITR Today,* designed using desktop publishing software and created just for an interview with ITR Corporation.

Adrian has arranged her work samples in a 14 x 17 multi-ring binder. She will also include extra resumes and multiple copies of the sample layout of *ITR Today* to leave with the people who interview her. Her cover letter and resume are reproduced on pp. 101 & 102.

Adrian Wilis

246 12th Street, Akron, Ohio 44362
(216) 998-6432

January 11, 1991

Mr. Marshall Doer
Director of Personnel
ITR Corporation
244 Albany Avenue
Cleveland, Ohio 41432

Dear Mr. Doer,

I wish to apply for the position of editor of *ITR Today*. When you study the enclosed resume, you will see that I possess many of the skills needed to write and edit a company publication, including:

- A degree in communications;
- Experience in writing, editing and publication design; and
- Familiarity with computer applications used in publications production.

Enclosed is a sample issue of *ITR Today* that I created using Pagemaker desktop publishing software. I believe this sample demonstrates my writing and design abilities —the same skills I hope to apply to writing and designing actual issues of your newsletter.

Next week I will call your office to see about the possibility of discussing the job with you. I would like to share with you my portfolio of writing samples.

Cordially,

Adrian Wilis

enc.

Adrian Wilis

246 12th Street, Akron, Ohio 44362
(216) 998-6432

Job objective

Seeking a position in public relations in order to use writing, editing and publication design skills.

Experience

Communications Consultant, American Insurance Agency, Akron, Ohio.
Gathered information and wrote quarterly issues of company newsletter. Completed 12 issues of the eight-page publication single-handedly from 1987-1990. Advised staff on writing and design of assorted insurance documents.

Publicity Coordinator, Akron PTA.
Coordinated all PTA events for Richardson Elementary School, 1988-1990. Wrote all promotional materials and distributed news releases to the media.

Writer, Cleveland State University Alumni Office.
Wrote and edited 14 recruiting publications for CSU during employment from 1979-1982.

Education/Training

B.A. Business and Organizational Communication, The University of Akron, 1979. GPA 3.2.

Completed 18 hours of training in use of Pagemaker desktop publishing software in 1990.

Professional

Member Akron Chapter of Women in Communications, 1979-1990.

Portfolio and references available.

Chapter 7

Any Questions?

Answers To The Ones I Hear The Most

Q. I'm a college senior currently putting together my first portfolio. As a high school student, I was editor for the school newspaper. Should I include samples from that period in my portfolio?

A. Probably not, unless the work you did was award-winning or outstanding in some way. As a college student, your portfolio should contain only your best and most recent work. Including work samples from your high school years might suggest to an employer that you weren't productive enough in college to create sufficient samples to fill your portfolio.

Q. During an employment interview, who should introduce the showing of the portfolio—me or the employer?

A. The employer usually likes to take control of the interview, so let him suggest the right time for viewing your work. You can, of course, make reference to your work and your portfolio when you answer the interviewer's questions. Your reference may logically lead to an invitation to show your work.

Q. I write for the college newspaper. One of my best articles has a typo in it that occurred during typesetting. Should I still include the article in my portfolio, even though it's not "perfect"?

A. Unfortunately, you won't usually have control over all stages of the production and printing of your work. Although in your case the typo is not your error, it is still a mistake that detracts from the quality of the writing. And if you correct the error with a pencil, your article will look messy. My advice: don't include the piece at all.

Q. I don't have enough work to fill a portfolio case. What should I do?

A. You can always create some pieces or you can "flesh out" your portfolio by including your resume, your transcripts, awards certificates (if the award is related to your field of study) and letters of commendation from supervisors and employers. Don't turn your portfolio into a scrapbook of your accomplishments, however. The majority of the pages should be filled with samples of your work.

Q. If I don't have enough work to fill my portfolio, what should I do with the blank pages?

A. Take them out of the binder. Blank pages emphasize to an employer that you don't have enough experience to fill a portfolio. Although that certainly may be the case, you don't want to call attention to the fact.

Q. Should I include explanatory tags in my portfolio?

A. The portfolio is an interview tool. If, as is usually the case, you will be presenting your portfolio in person, then you can explain your work during the interview. In that situation, explanatory tags would be redundant. But if you are mailing or dropping off your portfolio, then you certainly will need to include some explanatory tags. Prepare the tags, but only put them into the portfolio when you will not be around to explain your work face to face.

Q. I've done a lot of script writing. Should I present my scripts as audiotapes or as typewritten copy?

A. Include both formats in your portfolio.

Q. Should I present my published work as photocopies or tear sheets?

A. Present the tear sheets unless they're too large for the portfolio page, or if you don't have a clean, attractive original tear sheet.

Q. As a photographer, I've included my best black-and-white prints in my portfolio. How do I present my work to out-of-town employers who are asking to see my work?

A. Make slides of your prints. Mark each slide with your name, address and copyright notice. Mail the slides in a transparent, vinyl-pocketed sheet suitable for viewing over a light table. Be sure to include a self-addressed stamped envelope (with sufficient postage) for the safe return of your slides.

Q. As a photographer, I have mostly slides in my portfolio. Should I call ahead to make sure each interviewer has viewing equipment, or should I carry my own equipment?

A. It's pretty awkward to carry, set up and show slides via a projector and screen during an interview situation. You can call ahead to find out what viewing equipment the interviewer has available; or you can carry your own hand-held slide viewer. Some photographers invest in small, portable desk-top slide viewers that are ideal to take to an interview.

Q. Many want ads for writers request that sample clips be sent with the resume and cover letter. Should I send original clips or photocopies?

A. Send photocopies. Save the original clips or tear sheets for your portfolio presentation.

Q. What kind of mounts should I use for my 35mm transparencies?

A. For a professional look, mount your slides in plastic mounts, which project a clean, sharp frame. Cardboard mounts, on the other hand, tend to project blurred edges, and glass mounts simply aren't suitable for some viewing equipment. If your slides come back from the photo lab in the standard cardboard mounts, you may want to remount them into plastic.

Q. I'm aiming at a career in fashion illustration. Should my portfolio contain illustrations in pen, brush and ink, wash, watercolor or pencil? How do I decide which media to use for my portfolio samples?

A. Your portfolio should show a variety of techniques and skills in the use of various media, because the needs of prospective employers and clients will vary. Arrange your portfolio samples to highlight your versatility as an illustrator—but also do your homework on the individual firms with which you will be interviewing. In the front of your portfolio, place the work most likely to interest a specific interviewer.

Q. Should I use both sides of the portfolio page to display my work, or just one?

A. Using both sides of the page gives an interviewer a sense of continuity. It also makes more efficient use of the viewer's time. Leave blank pages only if you want to give a sense of division between major parts of your portfolio—between samples that depict different subject matter, formats or media.

Q. I don't have a lot of money to invest in a portfolio case. Won't my work speak for itself, even if I present it in a shoebox instead of in an expensive case?

A. If your work is exceptional, it won't matter what kind of package you present to employers. You'll be hired on the merit of your work. But keep in mind that when you are competing with other similarly qualified applicants for the same job, it is often the candidate with the most professional presentation who wins the position.

You'd be wise to invest in a portfolio case. You needn't spend a fortune. You can purchase a simple, multi-ring binder, and upgrade to a more attractive case when you can afford it.

Appendix A

Professional Organizations

Where To Get More Information

Following is a list of professional organizations for communicators and visual artists.

Although this is by no means a complete listing of such groups, the organizations named here are particularly supportive of students in their respective fields.

Some sponsor educational programs or scholarships; several offer student memberships at a discounted dues rate.

Your college or university may even have student chapters of one or more of these organizations already established. Inquire at the Student Affairs or Career/Placement Center. (If not, you may wish to participate or take an active role in starting one.)

American Advertising
Federation
1400 K Street NW, Ste 1000
Washington D.C. 20005
202-898-0089

American Institute of Graphic
Arts
1059 Third Avenue
New York, NY 10021
212-752-0813

American Society for Hospital Marketing and Public Relations of the American Hospital Association
c/o American Hospital Assn.
840 North Lake Shore Drive
Chicago, IL 60611
312-280-6359

American Society of Magazine Photographers
205 Lexington Avenue
New York, NY 10016
212-889-9144

Art Directors Club
250 Park Avenue South
New York, NY 10003
212-674-0500

International Association of Business Communicators
870 Market Street—Suite 940
San Francisco, CA 94102
415-433-3400

National Association of Black Journalists
11600 Sunrise Valley Drive
Reston, VA 22091
703-648-1270

National Association of Government Communicators
80 South Early Street
Alexandria, VA 22304
703-823-4821

National Press Photographers Association
3200 Croasdaile Drive, Ste. 306
Durham, NC 27705
919-383-7246

Public Relations Society of America *and* Public Relations Student Society of America
33 Irving Place—3rd Floor
New York, NY 10003
212-995-2230

Society for Collegiate Journalists Institute of Journalism
CBN University
Virginia Beach, VA 23463
804-424-7091

Society of Illustrators
128 East 63rd Street
New York, NY 10021
212-838-2560

Society of Professional Journalists
Sigma Delta Chi
53 West Jackson Bl., Ste. 731
Chicago, IL 60604
312-922-7424

Women in Communications, Inc.
2101 Wilson Blvd.—Suite 417
Arlington, VA 22201
703-528-4200

Appendix B

Getting An Informational Interview

An Especially Useful Assignment

Assignment: Prepare a report that informs the reader about an entry-level position as a (name the position) at (name the company).

In order to complete the assignment, you must make contact, by letter, phone or in person, with someone currently working in the career field in which you are interested. This type of *informational interview* should give you a good idea about your career choice and what it would be like working for a specific company that employs people with skills similar to yours.

The interview will also provide you with at least one important professional contact in the field, the start of your own networking list.

Be careful when setting up your interview to tell the professional that you are only seeking career information, that you are *not* yet seeking a job. This will put him or her at ease—no hiring decisions today, thank you—and make it easier for you to carry on an informal discussion and get exactly the detailed information you need.

This assignment can be done as a career exploration exercise; or the topic(s) can be thoroughly researched from both primary (interviews) and secondary (printed materials) sources in order to produce a documented research paper.

You can even include the assignment in your portfolio to show that you know how to research a career and an industry.

Be sure to write a thank-you note to the professionals that give you the information you need to complete this assignment.

Appendix C

Company Information Resources

Don't Forget The Library!

One of the best sources of information about a publicly held company is the firm's annual report. Many libraries keep current annual reports on file; at some libraries, this information can be accessed via a computer database. Ask the business librarian about your library's holdings, or write directly to the company for a current annual report.

Another good source of company information is an interview with a current employee in the career field of interest (see Appendix B). Try to obtain copies of the company's internal publications (employee newsletter, benefits brochure, etc.) when you conduct an informational interview of this type.

The following sources of company information may also be helpful. Most are published annually and can be found in the reference section of your library:

- *The Career Directory Series* (The Career Press)
- *College Placement Annual*, College Placement Council
- *College Placement Directory* (Zimmerman & Lavine)

- Dun and Bradstreet's *Million Dollar Directory* and other corporate directories
- *Encyclopedia of Business Information Sources*
- *F&S Index of Corporations and Industries*
- Fitch Corporations Manuals
- *Forbes* magazine (Annual Directory Issue)
- Moody's Manuals
- *MacRae's Bluebook*
- *Standard and Poor's Corporate Records*
- *Standard & Poor's Register of Corporations, Directors and Executives*
- *Thomas Register of American Manufacturers*

Appendix D

Job-Hunting Books

More Help In Your Job Search

Occupational Information From the U.S. Department of Labor

America's 50 Fastest Growing Jobs
Extracts the 50 hottest job opportunities in the U.S. today and provides the who, what, when, where—and how-to—in seeking out these career paths.

The Dictionary of Occupational Titles
Names and describes over 20,000 occupations.

The Guide for Occupational Exploration
Groups occupations by interests, abilities and traits required for workers' success in each occupation.

The Occupational Outlook Handbook
Information on all occupational areas—nature of the work, working conditions, employment, training and qualifications, job outlook and earnings.

Other Career References

American Almanac of Jobs and Salaries, by John Wright, Avon, 1987.

Job descriptions and salary ranges for positions at government, corporate and professional employers.

The Career Directory Series, edited by Ron Fry, The Career Press, 1990.

Includes separate directories (featuring comprehensive job information) for careers in advertising, book publishing, business & finance, healthcare, marketing and sales, magazines, newspapers, public relations, radio & television, travel & hospitality. Updated biannually. (New editions in Spring, 1992)

College Placement Annual, College Placement Council, Inc.

Gives information on jobs offered to college graduates by corporate and government employers. Updated annually.

Encyclopedia of Careers and Vocational Guidance, edited by William E. Hopke, J.G. Ferguson Publishing Co., 1987.

Three volumes. Gives advice on how to plan for a career in a variety of fields; details each occupation according to nature of work, educational requirements, history, method of entry, advancement opportunities, employment outlook and earnings.

From Campus to Corporation, by Drs. Steven Strasser and John Sena, The Career Press, 1990.

The most up-to-date job-search guidebook written exclusively for college students and recent graduates—highly readable, eminently practical.

How to Survive Your First 90 Days at a New Company, by Paul Kaponya, Career Press, 1990.

Down-to-earth advice any "new hire" needs: the do's and don'ts that will spell victory or defeat at a new company, often in a matter of days.

Internship Series, edited by Ron Fry, The Career Press, 1990.

Includes three applicable volumes: Volume 1 (advertising, marketing, public relations and sales); Volume 2 (newspaper, magazine and book publishing); and Volume 5 (radio and television broadcasting and production). Features articles from top industry professionals and extensive listings of companies that offer internships, with names of contacts, application deadlines and procedures, qualifications, pay, etc. Updated biannually.

The Resume Guide for Women of the '90s, by Kim Marino, Tangerine Press, 1990.

The equalizing opportunity women have been searching for. Includes 50 resume samples, a lengthy list of action words, cover letter and thank-you letter samples and interviewing techniques.

The Resume Solution, by Dave Swanson, Jist Works, Inc., 1990.

Reveals secrets on resume design and printing, and offers job search and interviewing techniques as well. A results-oriented book.

The Right Job For You, by M. Michael Farr, Jist Works, Inc., 1991.

A step-by-step process helps readers identify their values and priorities, review and recognize the value of their experiences, identify their strengths.

Salary Success: Know What You're Worth...And Get It, by Drs. Ron and Caryl Krannich, Impact Publications, 1990.

Many employees receive 10 to 30 percent less than they could be getting. This won't happen to readers of this book! Includes assessment devices, self-directed exercises, handy reference guide to salary ranges for hundreds of jobs.

The Student's Guide to Finding a Superior Job, by William A. Cohen, Slawson Communications, Inc., 1987.

Some useful job-finding techniques for graduating college students.

Transitions: Successful Strategies From Mid-Career to Retirement, by Drs. Strasser and Sena, Career Press, 1990.

The companion volume to ***From Campus to Corporation.*** Excellent information on moving from non-manager to manager, from working married to working divorced, much more.

What Color is Your Parachute?, by Richard Bolles, Ten Speed Press, 1990.

Practical advice on job-hunting and ways to improve your chances of getting whatever job you go after. Updated annually.

Where The Jobs Are: A Comprehensive Directory of 1200 Journals Listing Career Opportunities, by Feingold and Hansard-Winkler, Garrett Park Press, 1990.

A unique "must" book for job hunters—lists where jobs are advertised in hundreds of fields.

Writer's Market, Writer's Digest Books, 1990.

From the publishers of ***Photographer's Market*** and ***Artist's Market.*** Depending on your speciality, one of these is a mandatory addition to your bookshelves.

Your First Interview, by Ron Fry, The Career Press, 1991. Advice on how to turn the interview into a job-winning experience—the first (and only) interview book written exclusively for college students and recent graduates.

Your First Resume, by Ron Fry, The Career Press, 1989. Targeted to college students and anyone else entering or reentering the job market; features sample resumes and letters.

Appendix E

Sources

Used In Writing This Book

Chapter 1

Fry, Ronald W., *Your First Resume: The Essential Comprehensive Guide for Anyone Entering or Reentering the Job Market,* Hawthorne, New Jersey: The Career Press, 1989.

Lewis, Adele, *How to Write Better Resumes*, New York: Barron's Educational Series, Inc., 1983.

Chapter 2

Fry, Ronald W., editor, *Internships, Vol. 1: Advertising, Marketing, Public Relations & Sales,* Hawthorne, New Jersey: The Career Press, 1990.

Fry, Ronald W., editor, *Internships, Vol. 2: Newspaper, Magazine & Book Publishing,* Hawthorne, New Jersey: The Career Press, 1990.

Fry, Ronald. W., editor, *Internships, Vol. 5, Radio & Television Broadcasting & Production,* Hawthorne, New Jersey: The Career Press, 1991.

Fry, Ron, *Your First Interview,* Hawthorne, NJ: The Career Press, 1991.

Jobst, Katherine, editor, *Internships '89,* Cincinnati, Ohio: Writer's Digest Books, 1988.

Occupational Outlook Handbook, U.S. Department of Labor, 1988-89.

Stanton, Michael, "Cooperative Education: Working Toward Your Future," *Occupational Outlook Quarterly,* Fall 1988, pp. 22-29.

Chapter 3

Burack, Sylvia K., editor, *The Writer's Handbook,* Boston: The Writer, Inc., 1989.

Conner, Susan, editor, 1989 *Artist's Market,* Cincinnati: Writer's Digest Books, 1988.

Eidenier, Connie Wright, editor, 1989 *Photographer's Market,* Cincinnati: Writer's Digest Books, 1988.

Neff, Glenda Tennant, editor, 1989 *Writer's Market,* Cincinnati: Writer's Digest Books, 1988.

Occupational Outlook Handbook, U.S. Department of Labor, 1988-89.

Rivers, William L. and Work, Alison R., *Free-Lancer and Staff Writer,* 4th Edition, Belmont, California: Wadsworth Publishing Co., 1986.

Standard Rate and Data Service Business Publications Rates, Standard Rate and Data Service, Inc., monthly.

Chapter 4

Craig, James, *Graphic Design Career Guide,* New York: Watson-Guptill Publications, 1983.

Paetro, Maxine, *How to Put Your Book Together and Get a Job in Advertising,* New York: Hawthorn Books, 1979.

Chapter 5

Bolles, Richard Nelson, *What Color is Your Parachute?* Berkeley, California: Ten Speed Press, 1988.

Standard Rate and Data Service, Standard Rate and Data Service, Inc., monthly.

The Perfect Portfolio